Are They *Really* Reading?

To struggling readers everywhere—those I've been fortunate enough to teach, and those I have yet to meet—you are the reason I love what I do.

Contents

Foreword

For the last decade, I have been attempting to distinguish the subtle differences that exist between someone being a good teacher and being a great teacher. A few years ago, I discovered a book that moved my thinking in understanding both the art and craft of engaging teaching and learning. Lorri Neilsen's book, *A Stone in My Shoe: Teaching Literacy in Times of Change,* teased out several characteristics I believe truly great teachers share: they ask "what if" questions; when there are stones in their shoes, they question the status quo; they immerse themselves in professional communities; *and,* they accept "perceived knowledge as provisional." Jodi Marshall is just this kind of teacher and learner.

Shortly after I moved to Florida to accept a teaching position at the university, a personable young woman appeared in my office wanting to know if I thought it would be possible for her to get a graduate degree in education while still keeping her hectic job. Although I had some initial doubts about the feasibility of matching her erratic work schedules with course offerings and internship requirements, Jodi's intense commitment quickly allayed my fears. She asked questions, examined all her options, and then made plans that would move her toward her goal. Those same characteristics not only helped Jodi overcome her education obstacles, but they also have made her an incredible teacher and researcher.

Jodi began her teaching career in the Orange County Literacy Project. She used the design of the literacy project as a model for her first classes. It wasn't long before Jodi noted that her classroom didn't always function the way the "model" suggested it should. Jodi defined success not in terms of an orderly classroom (although hers was) but in terms of whether students were actually becoming more competent and confident readers and writers because of the teaching moves she was making. As a new teacher, I'm sure there were many stones in Jodi's shoes, but the one that nagged at her the most was sustained silent reading time. As her confidence grew, Jodi began to see the "perceived knowledge" of the professional community as provisional until she could document that the time and practice were making a difference in the literate lives of her students.

Jodi's book, *Are They* Really *Reading?,* takes you on a journey of teaching self-discovery as she examines this stone in her shoe. She shares with the professional community her passion for wanting to use each minute of her time with children in ways that would really make a difference. She builds her own knowledge base and then takes us back to her students so we can see how their voices can and should change our thinking. When she changes schools, she helps teachers and administrators rethink their practices based on her new understandings. The stone gets moved into others' shoes.

Our professional community is fortunate to have this new voice—a voice reminding us that, especially in times of mandates and standards, it is still important to question the status quo. I have had the good fortune of seeing Jodi in her own classroom with her students. She loves to teach, and she loves to learn. *Are They* Really *Reading?* will take you into the classroom I visited. You will hear students' voices and share in their collaborative struggles. Jodi's students will remember her not as a teacher but as a *great* teacher. Her journey will remind each of us to value the struggle.

Dr. Janet Allen

Acknowledgments

I believe I wanted to be a writer long before I wanted to be a teacher. Growing up, I never really imagined myself teaching. I certainly never anticipated I would love it as much as I do. And I never thought that I could actually be a teacher *and* a writer.

In writing this book, I hope to provide teachers with realistic, successful strategies they can use to motivate students to read in their own classrooms by providing an honest glimpse into my own room.

Through the course of writing this book, I found myself filled with mixed emotions. I am sure my feelings are not unique: the sadness I felt when the writing experience was almost over, jubilation when it actually was over, and the fear that nobody would choose this book, or that people would choose it, but not read it, or that they would read it and not like it.

Throughout my roller coaster of emotional stages consisting of worry, confidence, sleeplessness, numbness, frustration, excitement, fatigue, and joy, I was fortunate to be surrounded by wonderful people who offered encouragement and support. Although many people contributed to this endeavor, I would like to express my sincere gratitude to the following individuals:

Thank you to Philippa, Bill, Brenda, and all the people at Stenhouse for making my dream of writing a book a reality. You each made the process smooth and pleasurable. I truly appreciate your humor, patience, tact, and encouragement.

My first principal, Dr. Katherine Clark, took a chance and hired me as a graduate student who had never taught middle school. Kate, I appreciate your support, trust, and continued friendship.

I met many staff members at Ocoee Middle School in Ocoee, Florida, who helped me as a beginning teacher. Thank you to Evelyn, Judy, Shawn, Craig, Debbie, Sharon C., Sharon G., Molly, Rich, and especially Dina. You made me love working in such a dynamic environment!

Anne Gibson, formerly the principal at Will Rogers Middle School in Lawndale, California, has always been honest and straightforward with me. She always went out of her way to accommodate my countless questions and requests. Anne, it was a pleasure to work for you. Thank you for believing in SSL and in me.

Martha, David, and Karen, you all became the new administration after the initial implementation of SSL. Thank you not only for keeping it intact, but also for continuing to support it. I appreciate the many details you tend to, from purchasing folders, to recruiting guest readers. Thank you for giving SSL a chance.

Many special people at the Lawndale Elementary School District in Lawndale, California, have helped me in various ways. Thank you to Dorinda, Evelyn, Liz, and Sue. You taught me the true meaning of professionalism. I am also extremely grateful for the opportunity to work with our team of reading specialists. You all make Thursday meetings educational, worthwhile, and enjoyable.

Each summer I work as a facilitator of literacy workshops in various schools across the country. The team I work with is truly phenomenal. Although I dearly missed time with you last summer while writing this book, please know how much you rejuvenate me. Jill, Lee, Christine, Kyle, Mary, Becky, Lee Ann, Steve, Beth, Julie, Anne, and Donna, you are each an inspiration to the teaching community and to me.

Many staff members at Will Rogers Middle School have made the schoolwide SSL program an enjoyable experience. Aida, Debbie, Donna, Moira, Stephanie, Tiffany, Delfina, Brent, and Joyce, thank you for your never-ending patience, hard work, and support.

There are also many teachers at Rogers whom I consider dear friends. Thank you to Dixie, my mom away from home who never tires of my constant requests for advice; to Al, for his straight talk and huge heart; to Donna, for her contagious laugh and spiritual support; to Margie and Dianne, who lift me up with kind words and smiles each and every morning; to Judy, for her wisdom and willingness to listen; to Steve, for his sense of humor and constant good-natured personality; to Leslie, for her infectious energy and sense of fairness; and to Wendy, for being an ultraorganized, supersensible, Velcro-crazy friend and colleague. I have learned so much from you all—thank you.

To my friends from Florida—Shari, Kim, Kelly, Jen, Dina, Caroline, and Kaären—the laughs, long conversations, weekly e-mails, and fun trips we share mean more to me than you'll ever know. Thank you for your constant, uplifting, ever present friendship.

My students at Ocoee Middle School and Will Rogers Middle School welcomed me as their teacher, but also acted as teachers to me. I have learned and continue to learn so much from all of you. Thank you for your patience, your willingness to try new things, your energy, your respect, and your contagious youthfulness. You fill my days with challenges, promise, laughter, and hope. You are the reason I look forward to coming to work each day.

I would especially like to thank Janet Allen. Janet, you are a true mentor, friend, and the person I want to "be just like when I grow up." Thank you for being such an inspiring role model. You have taught me so much about teaching, learning, living, and enjoying life. I can't tell you how meaningful and enriching it is to have someone like you in the teaching profession and in my life.

And to the most important people in my life, my family:

To Mom, Dad, and my brother Jeff—thank you for loving and supporting me and for shaping the person I am today.

To my husband, Drew—thank you for giving me friendship, unconditional love, and a life filled with laughter.

Introduction

I don't like reading. You don't have any good books to read. How long do we have to read? Can I go to the bathroom? Is time up yet?

I was hearing these types of comments from my students, and I heard them most often when they were supposed to be reading. They were making excuses and constantly asking to leave the classroom during our reading time. Some students kept misbehaving, hoping, perhaps, to get sent out of the room.

If these tactics sound familiar, your students probably aren't *really* reading in your classroom either. More than likely, they are struggling or reluctant readers, and they need more support from you before they can successfully participate in any kind of independent reading time. Like me, you might think sustained silent reading (SSR) is the answer.

During my first year of teaching middle school, I tried to make time for SSR in my daily schedule, but noticed after just a few months that my students were not enjoying it. I doubted whether they were reading at all. After talking to the students, and observing them, I realized that a traditional SSR program would not meet the needs of my struggling readers.

So I created a different reading program, one that goes beyond SSR, and it has far exceeded my expectations for promoting reading. I call it Supporting Student Literacy (SSL). SSL consists of three elements: sustained silent reading (SSR), sustained silent writing (SSW), and reading aloud (RA). There are many advantages to using SSL over a traditional SSR program. The combination of reading, writing, and reading aloud alleviates the monotony that often accompanies five consecutive days of reading, and allowing time for students to write provides emergent writers with a stress-free, nongraded time to experiment with style and format. Providing time for students to hear material read aloud to them can hook even your nonreaders. Reading aloud is by far the most important element I added to create SSL. Hearing short stories, poems, newspaper and magazine articles, and excerpts from books provides the spark struggling readers need to explore reading on their own. Exposing students to different genres is also an effective way to get them interested in material they might not otherwise select.

The best component about SSL is that you can start it right in your own room, and you don't have to be a "reading" teacher to make it work. You do need to encourage talk, rather than insist on complete silence, though, and you will need to hold quick conferences with students during SSR to help them choose books and talk about what they are reading. Later, as you watch your students transform into genuine readers, you can participate by simply modeling SSR. Be warned: the dramatic increase in reading on the part of the students will demand a wealth of appropriate reading material, which I discuss how to acquire in Chapter 3.

I experimented with SSL in my classroom in Florida for three years and found the results extremely promising. I noticed changes in students' attitudes immediately. I read a lot of young adult literature myself so I was able to recommend books to students. I also read numerous selections aloud each week as a way to increase their motivation to read, and I continually encouraged them to share their own book recommendations. I wanted my students to know that I valued literacy and that I could easily enjoy the same books they did. Students started entering my room early, often eager to share their latest book with me. They did not try to pack up their belongings before the bell, but continued to read until it rang. I also rarely heard that question teachers dread: "How much more time is left before we get out of here?"

I talked to students frequently about SSL, asking for their opinions and suggestions. When I asked if they liked the reading days, Stephanie, a seventh grader, replied, "I love this time! I read so much more now. This is the first class I have ever had where I can talk about books to other people!" Apparently, though, too much questioning can be bothersome to the students. Once when I checked in with a different student, he said, "Will you please stop worrying about whether we are happy, and just let us read? THAT would make us happiest of all."

Just as SSL was really beginning to flourish, my upcoming nuptials required me to relocate to Los Angeles. When I was hired as the reading specialist for a middle school there, the principal asked me for suggestions for improving their schoolwide traditional SSR program. After sharing the successes I had had in my previous classroom, we decided to use my SSL program throughout the school. The results have been truly exceptional. Although it was an enormous undertaking, students and teachers now share positive attitudes about reading and writing. Students are eager to read aloud and are willing to share their reading and writing. Our school comprises approximately 1,100 seventh- and eighth-grade students. After participating in only two consecutive years of SSL, the class of 2000 increased their reading comprehension scores on our state-standardized test by more than 40 percent! When we celebrated Read Across America (the birthday of Dr. Seuss) with a "read-in," three times as many students volunteered to be guest readers than had volunteered the previous year. Several students even complained that the library was getting "too crowded and cramped" during lunchtime.

All the comments students shared with me were positive, and I genuinely thought the school was becoming a community of readers through SSL. It is clear to me that the mood I was sensing from talking to the students was consistent with our test results. Students were enthusiastic about SSL and were demonstrating a willingness to improve in reading and writing.

In this book, I describe all the tools necessary to implement SSL in your own classroom or school. I am amazed at the progress I see each day as the program continues to succeed. I am confident that you, too, will experience the thrill of creating lifelong readers through SSL.

CHAPTER ONE

Are They Really Reading During SSR?

What kind of reader are you, David?

    I dunno.

    When we have shared reading, and I am reading aloud and you are following along, are you a reluctant reader or a struggling reader?

    Umm . . . I'm not sure.

When we read together like that, do you have difficulty with the reading?

Not really.

When you are reading a textbook in your science or history classes, is it hard for you?

Uh, I guess. I'm not sure.

When we have sustained silent reading, and you are reading by yourself, what kind of reader are you?

Well, I don't always get to reading too much.

What do you do if you aren't reading?

Well, I sorta thought this was our free time, you know, as long as we were quiet.

I was having a conference with David, a seventh-grade student, during sustained silent reading to find out what kind of reader he considered himself. I wanted the students to think about the type of reading they were being asked to do in a typical school day and then determine how they tackled the reading in each instance. I was talking with David alone so he would feel comfortable enough to be honest in his answers without worrying about what the other students might say. I also wanted the students to enjoy reading for pleasure, but I wasn't sure how to find out if they were. What I found out from talking to David, and later from conferences with other students, is that they *weren't reading* during sustained silent reading time. Although the conversation with David continued, I didn't get much further with him or the other students. I was a first-year teacher armed with an arsenal of newly learned strategies, none of which I had ever actually used with a class of my own students. Yet I was eager to try them all out, as new teachers often are, and creating a silent reading period was my first weapon of choice. I set aside ten minutes each day for students to read silently and independently. I didn't want to start off with too much time because I was trying to be realistic about how "sustained" the reading would be with at-risk middle school students. *How hard can it be to get students to read for a mere ten minutes?*, I thought. How wrong I was!

What Kind of Class Is This?

It was my first teaching assignment and I was hired to be the sixth-, seventh-, and eighth-grade language arts teacher at a low-performing middle school in a low-income area in rural Florida. The school consisted of approximately 1,400 sixth-, seventh-, and eighth-grade students, almost 90 percent of whom qualified for free or reduced-price lunch. I was one of ten teachers piloting a literacy project classroom that was new to my county. My classes consisted of two-hour blocks of time with the lowest-performing students in each grade. Most students were recommended to be in my class by other teachers. (I am sure you can imagine what types of students were given to the new, first-year teacher who had asked for all the students who needed help in reading.) I checked student files and confirmed that I would have the students who did indeed have the lowest test scores in our school on the reading comprehension portion of our state-standardized test. Other teachers knew many of my students because they had been retained in previous years, or were notorious for their antics during summer school or in-school suspension. Several students were considered academically at risk or had behavior problems, and many had poor attendance records.

I was fortunate enough to finish creating the list of the identified students before the start of the school year (with just two days to spare). I called each student to explain what the literacy classroom would be like, and to make sure I had the support of the parents. I also wanted the students to know that they would not get a traditional elective like band, computers, or art if they took my class. The students agreed to be in the class, but without much enthusiasm. Most parents were either quietly stunned by the news of a new two-hour reading class, or appreciative that their child was selected. But there were a few exceptions. I remember one conversation with a mom who told me, "I flat out do NOT want my child to have all work and no fun in these middle years. Don't put him in if he won't get band."

My job was to act as the students' language arts and elective teacher. To reach all grade levels, I was asked if I would teach one block of sixth grade, one block of seventh grade, and one block of eighth grade, which would leave me with no planning period. It was a grueling schedule for a first-year teacher, especially because I was also pursuing a graduate degree that year, but I accepted. Luckily, I had the much-needed support of an adviser, who was also my professor at the time; my principal; the staff at my school; and personnel from the county office. I was observed and "dropped in on" so much that the first-year teacher observations became a breeze. Administrators visited regularly to see how the "new program" was coming along. County personnel also came in routinely, because the program was a pilot program. Although it was in only ten schools at the time, it was being considered for our entire district. To date, I believe they now have those literacy project classrooms in more than 300 middle and high schools. The county office had asked us to incorporate a computerized reading program developed by Vanderbilt University (which has since been purchased by Scholastic and is now called Read 180) into our daily schedule, so I also had monthly visits from the two creators of the program, who flew in from Tennessee. My graduate professor also came in to visit, observe, and offer suggestions. Although I found her presence immensely beneficial, it also had its drawbacks. I distinctly remember the time she decided to have a little fun with me and tell my class of students about my behavior as a student in her class. I had class with her weekly and we had recently participated in an exercise where we selected, read, and performed poetry. The purpose was to get us (the students) to look through a large number of different poetry books, ones we wouldn't select on our own, I suspect, and find one we liked. Then as a group, we had to perform the poem for the rest of the class, in any format we chose. Some students made the poem into a rap, some sang it as a song, several groups acted it out as a dramatic scene, and some groups (including mine) just simply read it. I liked the idea and asked my professor to come to my classroom the day I was trying it with my students. I can still remember the smirks on their faces as she said, "Just last Monday night, your teacher wouldn't volunteer to come to the front of the room to perform the poem her group was working on. Yes, your teacher was cowering in the back, hiding and hoping to not be seen. She wanted her group to go last, I guess. So you show her up and come on up to share your poems today!" As embarrassing as it was for me, it was actually a terrific way to get the students to see me in a more "human" light (because we all know that in students' minds, teachers aren't *real* people) and my relationship with my students was strengthened because of it.

I had done so much preparation to build a community in my classroom, and received so much feedback from my many observers, that when I wanted to start a daily silent reading period, I honestly thought I was well equipped. I had also taken several young adult literature courses in which I had read more than fifty young adult books. I purchased most of those novels, and thought I would have a great classroom library with which to start. As I said earlier, I thought it was important to start with a short amount of time, so I decided on ten minutes. I didn't want to scare the students away with too much time, but I wanted them to have enough time to read at least a few pages. I also searched used bookstores, garage sales, and friends' classrooms for picture books and books on tape, so that some of the less-skilled readers would be able to read something independently during the period. I scheduled the reading time for the beginning of our two-hour block.

I had already designed my classes to start with a "warm-up" each day. Every day, in the same place on the board, I wrote instructions for the opening activity. Previously, warm-ups had consisted of something short and simple such as unscrambling words, a word wall question, a brainteaser, a riddle, a quote, or sentences that needed to be corrected. The remaining part of the class had been spent on shared reading, learning stations, and, on certain days (usually Fridays), writing workshop. The learning stations had consisted of time for guided reading, conferences, vocabulary work, grammar mini-lessons, running records, writing strategies, or some other lesson or strategy that would aid comprehension of our shared reading book. To start the reading program, I thought it made sense for each day's warm-up to be simply written directions instructing the students to get their independent reading books and start reading silently. Because I had a class of students who had all scored low on the reading comprehension portion of our state-standardized test (a stanine of one, two, or three, which is considered below grade level), I thought they would all need the same support. I really expected the implementation of a reading period to be quite easy. Trying to be a model teacher, I, too, read young adult books during this time, stopping when the class did, after about ten minutes.

When we first started this reading time, I thought it was working rather nicely. The room was quiet, students were reading, there weren't many complaints when they came in and I said it was time to start (although there weren't any when I asked them to stop reading, either), and the students seemed happy. When we stopped reading, I would use a group discussion format to ask informal questions about what they were reading, whether they liked their books, and if they had recommendations for others. I received mostly one- and two-word answers, but they *were* responding, and they seemed to be trying. Still, I did not think we were truly mastering the art of creating a sustained silent reading period in our classroom. Something was missing. No one was really going beyond simple answers to my questions, and conversations were not evolving as I had hoped. There was not much enthusiasm in the room, students didn't often offer to share what they were reading, and I didn't really feel like I was *doing* anything. In most cases, I believe learning can and often does take place while the teacher is merely a facilitator, but in this case, I didn't think I was even facilitating anything! I blamed myself. I didn't think I was helping my students, and although I didn't think I was harming anything, either, I felt that a lot of *nothing* was happening. I thought the students were reading during the time allotted and therefore becoming better readers. For a long time I assumed that because the room was quiet, learning was taking place. I even complimented the class on their behavior during this time period, and was probably fooled more than once when students responded to one of my questions about a book when they hadn't even read it.

After months of the same scene in the classroom, (yes, I kept at it, exactly the same way for the first few months, hoping something would miraculously happen to change things for the better), I finally thought about making some changes. I decided to ask students more questions—deeper, more thought-provoking questions. I also asked them in a variety of ways—individually, in small groups, and in large groups.

I had a conference with Amber, a seventh-grade girl who was in the same class as David. When I asked her how she felt as a reader, she responded, "Pretty good." She was able to tell me that she felt like a reluctant reader in my class some of the time and a good reader at other times. Shared reading made her feel a little more successful than independent reading, but overall, she felt fairly confident. She told me she almost always struggled with the reading she had to do in other classes, especially textbook reading. It was there that she felt she was not a good reader, and she admitted she often did not do the reading that was assigned. The earlier conversation with David was an example of a conference that helped me see that things were not working. This conversation with Amber showed me that some students were reading and could make valid self-assessments. Given such varying degrees of engagement, I knew I needed to make some changes to ensure the success of *all* students. I wanted all my students to be aware of their reading abilities so they could better understand what strategies to use. What I learned was that many of them did not know how to reflect on their reading because they had not been reading. I knew a lot of research focused on giving students time to read, and I had been trying to do that—but I realized I had not really given them the tools they needed to make that time useful. I had very little in place during sustained silent reading that allowed me to determine whether they were, in fact, reading. I also had not considered that five days of consecutive sustained silent reading could become too tedious for at-risk middle school students. Setting aside time to read without providing the amount and variety of books necessary did not foster success. I also did not count on the vast difference in reading abilities. I had no idea that a student with a reading comprehension stanine score of one might be able to read only Dr. Seuss independently, whereas a student who had scored a three might be able to read Judy Blume. I had not even helped my students select books, but rather, put some out there and expected them to know what to choose. I continued to observe and reflect on my program to uncover the following concerns and observations.

Are They *Really* Reading?

Students appeared to be reading, but I could not tell if they were *really* reading or comprehending anything. By modeling literate behavior and reading myself, I could not walk around the room to watch students very closely. I do think teachers should read during a silent reading period, but I do not think you can start that way on the first day. There is no way to help the students choose the right book, watch them choose books, observe their behaviors, talk with them about what they are reading, read to them, or listen to them read if you are at your desk behind a book. I realized that these were the things my program was lacking. Common sense told me to read less at first, so I could observe and help them more.

What Kind of Conversations Should We Have About Reading?

I realized I was not asking the right questions to discover what I needed to know about the students' reading habits. Too often, I was asking questions that made them feel as if they were being "tested." Although I tried to keep the tone light and informal, most of my questions required yes or no answers, and therefore did not foster elaborate responses. I was also not asking the questions in the right format. Many students were not comfortable contributing to conversations about the books in a whole-group setting. Students who were reading picture books, because they were not yet skilled enough to tackle chapter books alone, were too embarrassed to share what they were reading. It was still the beginning of the year when I started this reading period, and we had not yet created the comfort level needed to get kids to share without fearing typical middle school ridicule. I also found that not all students were as honest as David or Amber, and appeared to be less than truthful about whether they were reading, what they were reading, and whether they were enjoying it. Some students gave the answers they thought I wanted to hear. I needed to find a way to get them to express their real thoughts and opinions.

How Do I Increase Motivation?

I didn't think the reading period was motivating enough. I hadn't had any discussions with the students about why they should read, or how it would benefit them. There was no incentive for reading, and since I was working with students who couldn't read on grade level, or did not like to read, I began to wonder if they might need one. At the same time, I struggled with that concept because I wanted the students to want to read for the sake of reading—not for a tangible reward. I also noticed that students were no longer coming into the room excited. When the warm-up was simple, like a brainteaser, students hurried into the room, eager to see if they could solve it. Since I had changed the warm-up to silent reading, they just entered the room quietly, and without the energy I had witnessed before. I began considering assigning a grade for our reading period, but was unsure how to do so without making it seem punitive. Since I was already giving points for almost every activity we engaged in, I thought about also giving points for this reading period. Remembering the need for constructive conversations in my classroom, I first asked the students how they felt about it, and they all loved the idea. I did wonder, though, if they liked it only because they thought they would be earning points for what they considered "free time." I decided we would have points, but was unsure exactly how it should be weighted.

Should I Hold the Students Accountable?

I had a good relationship with the students, and therefore, thankfully, had very few discipline problems. I was able to provide a safe, casual environment so they would not feel threatened or pressured by me or anyone else in the room. For the reading period, the students started reading when they entered the room, and I stopped them after ten minutes, followed by two minutes of not-so-great conversation. They did not have to respond to the reading, they were not getting a grade for reading, and I never "punished" anyone if I saw that they were not reading. Everything was very low maintenance and somewhat laid-back. No wonder the students felt this was free time—they really weren't responsible for anything. I actually overheard one boy tell a new student, "She [the teacher] likes to read every day. Just look like you're reading. It's only for ten minutes. It's easy!" I realized that he thought I was making them read just so *I* could read, and although I wanted them to know how much I liked to read, I did not want them to think that my personal enjoyment was guiding the curriculum. I needed to find a way to hold them accountable without making them (or myself) miserable in the process.

Establishing Expectations

Although I had been modeling reading, I never really discussed expectations with the class. I had not given them any guidelines before the start of the program so they would know what I wanted from them. My first goal was for them to find compelling literature that was pertinent to their lives, and enjoy reading it. I also wanted them to become better readers, thinkers, and communicators, building fluency and vocabulary along the way. I realized I should have held a roundtable discussion where I told the students why I wanted them to participate in a reading period and to find out what they wanted to get out of this time. Because I had not communicated any of that before starting sustained silent reading, the students did not know what to expect, and not all of them even had the same expectations. Most students viewed this period as free time, and it began to feel like free time, even to me.

Choosing the Right Books

Although I encouraged students to borrow books from me, very few books were being checked out. I took my classes to our school library several times, but they were not checking out books there, either. They simply were not interested in reading in class or at home. One of the worst things I did was give book talks without first researching the reading level of the students. I had given book talks on several books that *I* had enjoyed reading, but that were way too difficult for my students. Recommending books that I swore were compelling and captivating, only to have students try them and find them too difficult, really interfered with the trust I was trying to build. I felt terrible that I had unknowingly set them up to fail. I worried that they were giving up on reading, and I didn't want them to think I was giving up on them. I had not been able to find an abundance of high-interest literature written for low levels. I needed to make sure I could provide materials on a variety of topics, and at a multitude of reading levels. Margaret Mooney, author of *Reading To, With, and By Children,* says books should have "charm, magic, impact, and appeal." I needed to rethink the titles I was suggesting to make sure they matched the needs and interests of my students.

Through my classroom observations and from many conversations with my students, I realized I needed to make major changes to ensure reading success for all the students. From reading professional books by authors Janet Allen, Nancie Atwell, Lucy Calkins, Donald Graves, Tom Romano, and others, I thought I had a good understanding of how to develop a balanced literacy program. Although I was already doing that in my classroom, through the piloted literacy project format, I didn't think I was as effective as I could be. I was reading aloud to the students, they really enjoyed it, and we were having great discussions. We also had shared reading time together, which was incredibly successful. But my attempts at independent (sustained silent) reading were obviously not as effective.

In spite of that, and the fact that I had not yet tried guided reading, I felt we were flourishing in our endeavors to employ "reading to and with" on a weekly basis. Still, overall, things were not fitting together as I thought they should. Janet Allen, in *Yellow Brick Roads: Shared and Guided Paths to Independent Reading 4–12,* says, "An assessment measure for the effectiveness of read-aloud, shared reading, and guided reading is whether those approaches lead to engaged readers who demand independent reading time in school and choose to read outside school hours" (2000, p. 101). My students were definitely not demanding independent reading time, and were not taking advantage of the available time to engage in reading at home or in class. I decided to apply the same elements of a balanced literacy approach to my reading period that I already had in my weekly schedule, by making some significant changes to our SSR time. Instead of having sustained silent reading for five consecutive days each week, we would also add writing and reading aloud to our schedule.

Using Classroom Conversations to Guide Change

*In schools, talk is sometimes valued and sometimes avoided, but—
and this is surprising—talk is rarely taught. It is rare to hear teachers
discuss their efforts to teach students to talk well. Yet talk, like reading and writing, is a major motor—I could even say* the *major
motor—of intellectual development.*

Lucy Calkins, *The Art of Teaching Reading*

Conversations and Concerns

I decided changes needed to be made, but wanted to be careful and systematic in my approach. I knew that I needed to uncover the students' opinions and desires and that those ideas should guide the changes. Otherwise, the students would not have any ownership and the program would never work. The first thing I did was talk to the students about our reading time. I wanted to get their input before I told them how I had been feeling about the situation. I knew I would need their help in making changes, so I thought it best to make sure that I knew where they stood and that they knew they were being heard. I could then use their input, which ended up being remarkably similar to mine, to steer the changes I would make. I know now that I should have had those conversations with the class prior to the original beginning of our reading time.

Teaching Tip	Classroom conversation starters:
	■ Does anyone know what SSR stands for?
	■ How many of you have participated in SSR before?
	■ How did you like SSR?
	■ What did you like about it?
	■ What did you dislike about it?
	■ How did it help you become a better reader?

The tone you use when speaking to your students is more important than you might realize. Kids pick up on the slightest nuances. They often think they can determine how you feel about them by the tone you use and the amount of time you are willing to engage in conversation with them. Several students throughout the years have told me about the effect my conversational tone had on them.

One year, a student simply said, "Hey, you sure talk a lot."

My first reaction was to laugh, because to me, that sounded like an insult. I said, "Really? What do you mean?" "Well, you're always asking us stuff, and you always want to know more and ask us why all the time. No one else really does that, not even my mom!"

Other students have told me that I talk to them "more than any-one else during the entire school day." I now consider these types of remarks compliments, and I hope my tone makes the students see that I truly care about what they have to say.

Topics we discussed that year were the length of SSR, the books available, grading, motivation, the lack of enthusiasm, and the absence of accountability. Basically, we discussed all of the things I mentioned in Chapter 1 that I had hoped would happen during our reading time but that we had never discussed. I asked the students for suggestions on improving the quality of our reading time before I offered any input of my own. Once we identified the problems and, most important, discussed why they were concerns, we were ready to put our heads together to come up with solutions that would be agreeable to everyone. The topics the students most wanted to explore were as follows: the amount of time we had for SSR, the number and types of books available to them (or lack thereof), our "sharing" time, and grades. Issues that I wanted to think about and wanted them to be aware of were whether they were really reading during SSR time, the types of conversations we were having about the reading, building a better classroom library, how to increase motivation, establishing clear expectations, how to employ account-ability measures, and whether to assign a grade.

Time for SSR

After observing the extraordinary length of time my students took to select a book each day, I began to think that the ten minutes we had set aside for SSR was not enough time. Surprisingly, my students agreed. We talked about how difficult it is to come into a room, choose a book, start reading, and get into the book in only ten min-utes. The students agreed to try an extended period of fifteen to twenty minutes.

Books

The students informed me that I did not have enough books in my classroom library, nor did I have enough variety. However, they did not know enough titles or authors to give me suggestions. I passed out catalog pages (ones with pictures and summaries of the books) and asked students to mark the books they would be interested in reading. I also asked students to name the genres they usually liked to read. Then I vowed to try to buy at least ten new books.

Talking About Books

A clever mind is not a heart. Knowledge doesn't really care.
Wisdom does.
Benjamin Hoff, *The Tao of Pooh*

The students confirmed my fears when they told me they sometimes felt as if I was quizzing them at the end of our SSR time. They asked if I would talk to them individually instead of as a group. To my surprise, they also admitted that they would like help during SSR. One student said she would like it if I could help her sound out words and read some of her book aloud to her. Another complained, "You never ask about our books until the end. You're too busy reading your own book, I guess." I vowed to spend more time helping them choose books, asking about their book selections, reading to them, and listening to them read during SSR time, and less time modeling reading.

Grades

The students told me they wanted to earn grades (points) for the time they read in my room. They said I was willing to give points for every other activity or lesson done in my room, so it only made sense for me to give points for our silent reading time. When we talked about how to do this, one student suggested that I ask everyone to write a summary of what they had read each day. Another suggested that they tell me what their book was about when we had one-on-one sharing time, and another suggested they keep a simple record of the pages read. I liked the idea of them telling me what they read better than the idea of a written summary, but I also wanted some sort of record-keeping device. I was afraid that constantly requiring a lengthy written response might turn them off to reading (and writing), especially since some of them were not yet hooked on reading.

More Input

Knowing that students can sometimes open up even more if they are not responding in front of a group, I decided to give them a short, easy-to-complete, written survey taken from Janet Allen's *Yellow Brick Roads*. I thought this would help me uncover how they truly felt about themselves as readers and learners, and their attitudes toward reading and writing (see Appendix 2).

Students were given the surveys and asked to honestly write how they felt about literacy. I hoped the results would allow me to help them become more skilled and confident readers and writers.

For my class, reading the survey aloud before the students answered individually was essential. I often read directions, questions, or prompts from assignments to the students so they have an opportunity to ask questions and time to process what is being requested of them. Just giving them the surveys produced more in-depth class discussions. My students seemed shocked that I wanted to hear more of their opinions. I told them that they did not have to put their names on the survey, and that I would use their responses only as a way to improve our SSR time. They were then relaxed about completing them and responsive to discussions about them.

The results proved to be enlightening. Very few of my students considered themselves readers or even wanted to read, and only one student listed a favorite author. (She wrote Rodman Philbrick's name, and I have a feeling she knew his name only because our class happened to be reading his book *Freak the Mighty* at the time.) Almost all my students replied that they enjoyed it when people read stories to them, but did not like to volunteer to read aloud to others. Astonishingly, more than half of my students responded "sometimes" to the question "Do you expect reading to make sense?"

I had so few students answer "yes" when asked if people in their lives talked to them about reading, that improving our discussions and sharing sessions became one of my goals during our SSR time. Frank Smith in *Understanding Reading* calls a community of readers a "literacy club" and says that literacy should "float on a sea of talk" (1994). I believe that talking to your students about what they are reading is vital. Students need to feel comfortable talking about what they are reading, especially if we want them to make personal connections to what they read.

Since so many students had said they like to be read to, I thought it might be beneficial if part of our SSR time could be spent reading and sharing texts aloud. Margaret Mooney, author of *Reading To, With, and By Children,* also expresses this when she writes,

> Reading to children enables the teacher to demonstrate the nature, pleasures, and rewards of reading, and to increase children's interest in books and their desire to be readers. When children have frequent opportunities to hear stories, poems, rhymes, and chants read and sung to them, they become familiar with the ways language can be recorded, and they learn how stories work. Hearing stories from another perspective adds new meaning and impact to children's own thoughts and experiences. (1990)

Parental Input

I always strive to gain the support of parents or caregivers with whatever lesson or activity I am teaching, and this reading time was no different. In fact, I thought it might help to give the parents a short, simple survey asking them about their children's likes and dislikes (see Appendix 2). The survey had only ten questions and required only that parents check off appropriate answers. Unfortunately, only five surveys were returned to me that year. Nevertheless, I highly recommend creating such a survey in the hopes that you will receive greater feedback than I did.

If your class size will allow it, I also recommend calling parents instead of (or in addition to) sending a survey home. Hearing you ask specific questions about their student makes a parent more likely to support you. I found that when I called students' homes for reasons other than discipline problems, both the parent and the student appreciated it. Reasons to call might include the following: to ask about the student's interests or hobbies, to praise the student for appropriate classroom behavior, or to applaud the student for finishing a novel, completing a homework assignment, or scoring well on a test. If you are working with struggling readers, chances are this will be one of the few times the parent is given positive feedback. I recommend that you contact parents at least two times during each grading period to share something encouraging about their student. Just make sure that you are equitable with your calls, a lesson I learned the hard way.

It was the beginning of the year and I was calling parents for the first time. I wanted to be able to call every single parent and report something positive. I thought it was important to let them know that I would be communicating with them regularly, and that I expected their support. I also wanted them to know I would be sharing praises with them, not just problems. It wasn't difficult to find something positive to say, especially at that point in the year, but finding the time to make all the calls was extremely challenging. I was approximately halfway through my list when I noticed it was getting late. I decided it would be inappropriate to call at that late hour, and vowed to make the rest of the calls the next day. The day started off smoothly enough, but then around fourth period, a student came in bragging in the typical middle school sing-song voice, "Mrs. Marshall called my house last night and I didn't get in trouble. In fact, my parents were actually in a *good* mood afterward." Another child said, "Yeah, same thing for me." As more and more students admitted to each other that I had called, one boy stood up and yelled, "Hey, why didn't I get a good phone call? Or any phone call at all? What's up with that?"

Once I had all the input from my students and their parents, and the class had discussed the issues they felt were important, I wanted to address the topics *I* had been struggling with—the first being, "Are the students really reading?"

Are They Really Reading?

The man who does not read good books has no advantage over the man who cannot read them.
Ralph Keyes, quoting Mark Twain, *Nice Guys Finish Seventh*

I decided to hold an open, honest, direct, whole-group conversation on this matter. I simply said, "I have a feeling some of you are not reading during our SSR time, and I would like to find out why. No one will get in trouble. I just want to hear from you so I can try to help, so everyone will want to read. Can you tell me what exactly is happening during our SSR time?"

Students started raising their hands to speak, timidly at first, gradually with more enthusiasm, once they heard that others felt the same way they did. The first person to speak was a seventh grader named Eric, who said, "No offense, ma'am, but your books ain't no good for me." When I asked him to explain further, he said, "There aren't any I feel like I can read all at one time, all in a row, all on my own." Several other students said some of the books looked interesting, and my talking about them made them want to read them, but when they tried them on their own, they were too hard. Another student simply said, "None of them make sense!"

I realized that I had been right—the majority of the students were not reading—but I now knew the main reason was that I had provided them with books that were too difficult for them to read independently. Initially, I was upset with myself for failing to recognize and meet the needs of my students. After further reflection, I realized how amazing it was that the students had been honest enough to admit in front of an entire class that they had not been reading, and that the books were too hard for them. I was grateful that I was now aware of their concerns. I also thought this information could help me in two other areas: building a better classroom library and increasing motivation. I chose to look at this admission as progression toward our goals of becoming a safe, trusting classroom community rather than as a setback.

How Will You Know What to Look For?

How will you know if your students are really reading? I suggest that you actually ask them, as I did. But if you are wondering what to look for, these are the most common traits I noticed in my struggling, reluctant, and nonreaders:

■ *Avoidance:* You might have students who avoid reading by asking to leave the room, by putting their heads down, claiming to be sick, or saying they misplaced their books. These students may also skip your class on a regular basis, or be absent from school many times each month. If you have students who are always conveniently being sent to the principal's office at the exact time your reading period takes place, you can bet they are "avoiders." You need to capture the interest of these students while they are in your class so they won't want to leave. The best way to do this is through reading aloud. Make your read-aloud selections so entertaining they won't want to miss them!

- *Indifference:* These students don't care about reading or about listening to you read, and nothing makes them even want to try. They act like reading is something beneath them, something they know how to do, but just choose not to. Some of them may actually know how to read, but just don't like it. They may read at a level below the other students and be afraid of being teased about the books they choose. Or maybe they have never read a book that mattered to them—one that showed them reading can be pleasurable. You need to find captivating reading books for these students so they will like reading again. If you cannot make a match immediately, try using an audiobook. Because using a book on tape appears to require less effort than independent reading, these indifferent readers will be willing to try it. Before long, if you have selected wisely, they will be hooked!

- *Disruptive Behavior:* Do you have any students who are constantly in trouble? If you do, pay close attention to *when* they tend to misbehave. Is it during your SSR time? These students are just doing anything they can think of to draw your attention away from the fact that they can't (or don't like to) read. More often than not, these students want to read, but don't know how to ask for help. They have been exhibiting poor behavior during reading time for so long, it seems natural to them. When you first encounter these students, don't make a big deal out of their behavior. Wait them out and see what they do next. When you have conferences with them, ask them to read a paragraph or two from the book they have chosen. Once you have determined they need help, suggest lower-level books or get them started on audiobooks. Make a note of their reading behaviors to use for guided reading groups later in your class.

■ *Fake Reading:* Some students may act like they are reading, but are really just faking it. They enter your room quietly, get a book fairly quickly, sit down, open their books, and turn the pages as if they are reading. They look like they are reading. They even act like they enjoy it. Some students might even be able to talk intelligently to you about the book they are pretending to read. These students have probably even talked to enough other students to learn the plots. Again, you need to find out if they are really reading. Have these students read to you while others are reading silently. Suggest alternative books if they are reading ones that are too difficult, and again, try audiobooks.

Keeping Logs

The students themselves asked to receive points for reading, but I wasn't sure I needed or wanted a concrete way to monitor this reading time. I did not want them to think of SSR as an assignment, or a chore, nor did I want them to think I needed them to record pages because I doubted whether they were really reading. However, so many students were making their own logs, I decided to create a universal one. Sometimes, several students in different class periods were reading the same copy of one book. Because they could not each check this book out, they were having trouble remembering where they left off each day. I suggested using bookmarks, but often, from one class period to the next, these were lost, misplaced, or mysteriously moved. Then I had one student who, just getting hooked on formulaic writing, needed to keep track of which books she had read in a series. The first time I saw her jotting down a few notes after reading, she explained, "I just finished this book and only now realized I had read it before. I don't want to do *that* again!" Yet another student created his own record so he could "look back and see his greatness." Thus, we agreed to have an accountability piece and to have it in the form of a log (see Appendix 1). The students helped me create the log and I agreed to keep the spaces for responses or notes smaller, so it would not feel like an assignment. In fact, I never specified exactly what they had to put in those spaces— I wanted them to feel free to write whatever they chose.

Sustained Silent Writing

Writers write. We tell students: a writer is someone who writes a lot. We need to craft our daily schedules so young writers write on a regular basis.
Ralph Fletcher, *Craft Lessons*

I believe it is important to give my students time for uninterrupted, nonthreatening, nongraded writing. To help them become contributing literate members of our school and our society, I thought it was imperative to give them time to practice reading *and* writing. I approached the class about adding two writing days to our schedule, assuring them that the writing could be on any topic, and that it would not be graded. I explained how common it is for people to practice when they are learning a new skill. The best example, which I knew my students would relate to, is sports. If a young man or woman is trying out for a basketball team, he or she needs to learn how to shoot a free throw. To learn how to do this effectively, one must practice persistently. The coach can show the player the basic steps of shooting a free throw, but the player then has to practice, independently and often. I pointed out that reading and writing are no different. The students needed to practice constantly. After this reasonable example, they agreed to give SSW a try.

Reading Aloud

I used to read aloud to my students to get them to be good: "If you'll just be good this morning, I'll read to you after lunch." I thought of the read aloud as being like candy—the kids loved it, but it seemed not so good for them—like time away from what we should have been doing. I still think of the read aloud as something deliciously edible, only now I see it as a wonderful vegetable—something so good for us as a class that we need several helpings of it each day.
Katie Wood Ray, *Wondrous Words*

Adding time for reading aloud to my students was by far the most important change I made to my reading program. Hearing short stories, poems, newspaper and magazine articles, and excerpts from books was the spark they needed to start exploring reading on their own. Patricia Cunningham, coauthor of *The Teacher's Guide to the Four Blocks,* includes reading aloud in her self-selected reading (SSR) block. She believes that teachers should spend the first five to ten minutes reading aloud from a variety of genres, topics, and authors. This will help "build fluency, motivate students to read a wide variety of materials, and build confidence as readers" (2001). Jim Trelease, in *The Read-Aloud Handbook,* quotes from the 1985 National Institute of Education study *Becoming a Nation of Readers* when he reports, "The single most important activity for building the knowledge required for eventual success in reading is reading aloud to children. It should occur at home and at school, and is a practice that should continue throughout the grades". Katie Wood Ray, author of *Wondrous Words,* writes, "The read aloud as a predictable, ritualized classroom structure does so much work in a classroom community, and it nurtures our individual and shared identities as readers and writers in so many complex and interesting ways" (1999). Numerous other studies have proved the connection between independent reading and reading aloud, but my decision to include it in our schedule was based on the wants and needs of my particular students. When I asked them to vote on whether they wanted one of our days to be spent reading aloud, they unanimously voted yes.

Setting Up the New System: Defining Your Own SSR Program

Knowing some of the new parameters I wanted for my reading program, I decided to do a little more research about other sustained silent reading programs. I discovered that there was an abundance of research on this topic, and that programs varied quite a bit among states, districts, schools, and even classrooms.

Simply having time for silent reading during school hours is not a new concept. Numerous programs have existed under various titles. The most common terms are sustained silent reading or self-selected reading (SSR), drop everything and read (DEAR), stretch out and read (SOAR), and independent reading (IR). All of these terms really belong in a category called free voluntary reading (FVR). FVR is a term used by researcher Stephen Krashen that means "reading what you want to read, with no book reports, no questions at the end of a chapter, and not having to finish the book if you don't want to" (Pilgreen 2000). This is the essence of what most schools and classrooms are trying to implement. Sustained silent reading and self-selected reading are the two main types of free voluntary reading. The other programs are simply adapted versions of sustained silent reading. Janice Pilgreen, author of *The SSR Handbook,* found that

> sustained silent reading in its earliest form was originally based on the following six criteria:
> 1. Students select the materials to be read silently.
> 2. The teacher models by also reading silently.
> 3. The entire class, school, or department participates.
> 4. No records or reports are kept.
> 5. Students select one piece of reading material to read for the entire daily allotted time.
> 6. A timer is set for uninterrupted reading time. (2001)

Self-selected reading, most currently researched by Patricia Cunningham, Dorothy Hall, and Cheryl Sigmon in *A Teacher's Guide to the Four Blocks: A Multimethod, Multilevel Framework for Grades 1–3,* is different in that it includes accountability on the part of the student and teacher. The basic setup for their self-selected reading time is as follows:

1. The teacher first reads a selection aloud to the class.

2. Books are selected by the students (with occasional teacher help).

3. Students are given time to read.

4. Students are conferencing with the teacher either in small groups or one-on-one while the remainder of the class is reading silently and independently.

5. Students share what they have read with the entire group at the end of the reading time. (2001)

How do you know which program to choose? In my case, I originally thought that answer would be easy. After all, I had read a tremendous number of young adult books and had a master of arts degree in English education. I soon discovered I needed to know what these particular students needed, and no book or graduate degree could tell me that. I believe you have to know your students profoundly to really know what they need and want. I had listened to my students read to me individually, so I knew they could decode words and often had no trouble understanding what they were reading. They were not reading on grade level, though, and still needed practice reading silently, independently, and aloud. I wanted to find a way to incorporate all of those elements into a reading time that would be beneficial, enjoyable, and effective for us all. Since I had surveyed my classes extensively and held numerous group and individual discussions, I decided to try a combination of existing programs and came up with the following schedule:

Monday and Wednesday: Sustained Silent Reading (SSR)

Tuesday and Thursday: Sustained Silent Writing (SSW)

Friday: Read-Aloud Day (RA)

Now that I had the basics, I needed a name for this new reading time—and what program would be complete without yet another acronym as its title? I enlisted the help of my students and received numerous outlandish suggestions. We finally determined that our program would be called Supporting Student Literacy (SSL).

Now that our reading program had a name, I needed to establish criteria. Having discussed all of the concerns with the class, I was ready to set some guidelines that I thought would be agreeable to everyone. I believe, after reading about many variations of SSR, and studying the merits of my program, that the following five components are the most critical to any sustained silent reading program: a varied schedule, access to enticing books, students' ability to choose reading materials, a classroom environment conducive to reading, and a knowledgeable teacher.

The Schedule

I have found that most of my middle school students have very short attention spans. It is difficult to keep them focused on one particular task for any substantial length of time. Although they respond quite nicely to a routine, they still need a variation of tasks. For my at-risk struggling readers, a routine that they could become accustomed to, but that wouldn't bore them, was vital. For approximately twenty minutes each day, students would be reading silently and independently (on Mondays and Wednesdays), writing silently and independently (on Tuesdays and Thursdays), or listening to a selection read aloud or reading aloud to the rest of the class (on Fridays). This schedule would remain the same for the entire year. SSL would take place at the beginning of my language arts block every single day. I posted the weekly schedule prominently above the board, and I wrote the daily schedule on the board each day.

Establishing this simple schedule early and teaching the students that they could count on it helped immensely. I no longer had to waste time telling them when we were about to participate in silent reading. Having it be the first thing they did also helped with behavior management. It became easy and students knew what to do immediately upon entering my room. Again, the fact that I let them help choose that schedule (they voted on which days would be for SSR, SSW, and RA) gave them ownership and pride.

How Much Time Is Enough Time?

The decision you make about the amount of time you choose for SSR is an important one. Most SSR programs spend no less than ten minutes and no more than thirty minutes reading silently. The time you choose should be in that range, but the exact amount will depend on the types of students you teach. Students who already have a love of reading will most likely want a longer amount of time. Struggling readers might not be able to keep focused for thirty minutes. I suggest you start small and increase the time as needed. It is much easier to start a successful reading program with fifteen minutes than it is with thirty.

Keep in mind that to some students, especially struggling read-ers, time is a big deal. Make sure you are completely clear when explaining new schedules to students. When I first started teaching two-period blocks, I attempted to explain the schedule to the class. Apparently I was not specific enough when I told them they would be in language arts for two periods so they could get extra help in reading, writing, and other literacy skills. The first question at the end of my little synopsis of the syllabus was, "You mean we're so bad at reading and stuff, we need so much help that we have to sit through *two different periods* in a row of the *same exact class,* just so we'll finally get it?" As I said, be clear and careful when explaining and establishing your guidelines and schedules.

Study your students, observe their behaviors during reading time, and watch their reactions and interest levels when being read to aloud. Then choose the amount of time you give them based on what best meets their needs.

Building a Literate Classroom Environment

With the exception of a few students, it's usually not easy for even the most experienced teachers to bring students to want to care for the classroom environment.

Ralph Peterson, *Life in a Crowded Place*

My students work really well when they have a clear, consistent routine to follow. Because I wanted the transition to supporting student literacy to be as smooth as possible, I knew I needed to prepare the students and the classroom before we actually participated in it.

Practice First

Before we started SSL, I went through a few practice sessions with the students. I had the entire class watch as a smaller group of three to four students went through the routine for each day. Therefore, the class saw "rehearsals" for the three different SSL days (sustained silent reading, sustained silent writing, and read-aloud). As an example for our SSR days, I asked the small group to come in, get their portfolios, find a book, sit down, and start reading. I explained that students who did this quickly would get the opportunity to sit in our comfortable reading corner. Believe it or not, this worked. Sitting in the reading corner, especially on the beanbag chairs, became so coveted, we had to create a seating chart. If a student needed help selecting a book, he or she was to go to another classmate for a recommendation before coming to me. I asked students to do this to encourage discussions about books and reading. I also knew that students would value their peers' opinions much more than they would mine.

As an example for our SSW days, students practiced coming in, getting their portfolios, sitting down, and writing on any topic they wished.

On RA days, students were to simply come in and sit down quietly while waiting to hear the read-aloud for that day.

Modeling what to do on these days before actually starting the program helped immensely. Students were able to see what they would be doing, and could ask questions without distracting others. It was a wonderful way to prepare the students and make them aware of my expectations. We practiced SSL in this format for one complete week and followed the daily schedule, using different students for each practice session. As a way to lighten the mood, and to clarify expectations, I even had students (with whom I had consulted earlier) enter the room doing the wrong thing, so that we, as a class, could discuss what they should have done instead. This gave students a clear understanding of behaviors I would and would not tolerate. After our week of role playing, I thought we were ready to embark on a new adventure—SSL!

Access to Books

Books have always been friendly to me. When I was going to school in Harlem, books were the secret friends I brought home. When I had speech difficulties, which I had most of my younger life, I could communicate with books. Writing poems, stories, and eventually books came naturally, the way hanging out with people who like you comes naturally.
Lois Duncan, quoting Walter Dean Myers,
Trapped! Cages of Mind and Body

Perhaps the most fundamental part of any reading program is access to books. The students I taught did not own many books, nor did they have school or local library cards with which to check out books. I actually asked students to count the number of books in their homes as a homework assignment the first week of school. Sadly, only two students reported owning more than ten books. I knew that the best way to get them reading was to have the books accessible, and that the books would be most accessible if they were available during SSL time. This meant that I needed to increase the number and variety of books I owned to build a more effective classroom library.

Building a Useful Classroom Library

I originally thought I did have a good classroom library. I had filled it with young adult books I had been required to read in graduate school. I was proud of the fact that I really had read those books, enjoyed them, and could still remember the plots. I had created excellent study guides for them and thought my students would love them.

Although I started with what I thought was a decent collection, I did not have nearly enough books in my classroom to call it a library, nor did I have a large enough variety of reading levels and topics. I had books that I thought would interest the students, but most were on a seventh-, eighth-, or even ninth-grade reading level. My students were reading at the fourth- and fifth-grade level. Many of them did not have the means to go to a bookstore to purchase books, and the few who did had no interest in doing so. In fact, when I asked those students about buying books, they said they would rather spend their money on clothes or shoes. I saw a lot of them reading magazines (usually on wrestling or video games) and when I asked, they said they bought them at the 7-11, or a local liquor store. Only two students owned cards from the county library, which they said they received when their elementary classroom went on a trip there, and neither of them had used their card since.

I had been living by the *Field of Dreams* philosophy: "If you build it, they will come." I learned, at the expense of my students, how wrong that was. I now knew the importance of matching the texts to my students, and the value of leading my students to the books that were appropriate for them. (An explanation of how to match texts to students is in Chapter 4, "The Teacher's Role.")

Basically, I needed to buy more books and I wanted them in my classroom as soon as possible. Initially, I spent a lot of my own money. I had already used up the money teachers are given at the beginning of the year for "supplies," as well as exhausted all of the Title I money my principal was able to provide. Because I had promised the students earlier that I would try to buy at least ten of the books they had chosen from catalog pages, I first purchased fifteen with my own money. We still needed more, however, so I then quickly wrote (and fortunately was awarded) a grant from our PTA to purchase more books. I again asked students to make selections. To ensure that the choices would not be too difficult, I gave students a catalog that had illustrations, summaries, and titles of books appropriate for grades 4–8 (instead of the catalogs for grades 7–12). Next I went to the community for help. I wrote to our local newspaper, and was given a free two-month subscription. In addition, I begged for old magazines from local businesses, which resulted in a collection of about fifty magazines (approximately ten different titles). This was a good start, but I still wanted more. I knew I could not count on my students to bring their own books. They did not own any to bring! So, after asking your principal, using your own money, and searching the community, where else can you go to get books?

School and Local Libraries

My students did not have school or county library cards, and many of them did not even know where these libraries were. If you want a successful SSR program, one of the first field trips for the year should be to your library. I recommend doing this only after you have given some book talks, discussed different genres, and learned the interests and reading levels of your students. Otherwise, leading them to the library will be like leading them to your classroom library: they won't know what to choose.

Another option is to get them acquainted with the library before they actually go. You can do this by inviting the librarian to come to your classroom to speak. He or she might even be willing to give some book talks on new arrivals or old favorites. The librarian at my school makes a library orientation video and asks teachers to show it to students during the first week of school. This is a great way for students to visualize and learn about the library so that it's not so intimidating when they go on their own. They watch the video and learn the proper procedures for checking out books and returning them. My librarian also records book talks at the end of her orientation video so students will begin thinking about books they might want to read. Again, find out the interests and reading levels of your students first, before you have the librarian give a book talk. A bad or boring book talk can do more damage than you think.

If possible, take your classes to your local library. This will ensure that your students know where it is and what it has to offer, and that they all have a card with which to check out materials. My students had no idea that our library had current, up-to-date magazines and videos available to check out. One student said, "I thought they only had stuff for older people. I didn't know their magazines would be cool!" Some of them were so excited by the number and variety of magazines and videos available, they started begging their parents to take them on a monthly basis.

Libraries often have sales where they sell books for much lower than the retail price. Ask your librarian for a schedule of these sales so you can spread the word.

Again, you can invite a local librarian to your classroom if it is not feasible to take your students there. You can also ask for library card applications and have them available at your back-to-school night, open house, and/or parent conference days. A list of libraries in the area, with hours of operation and maps, is also helpful. Some libraries will even set up displays showcasing the books your school uses for required and optional reading. A display with your school's reading list and multiple copies of the books you are recommending goes a long way toward helping students form good reading habits.

You can certainly check out books from the school or local library yourself and store them in your class for the time allowed. However, be aware that you can usually keep books only about two weeks. It may be difficult to keep track of those books, especially if you let students check them out, and it may not be convenient to keep making those trips to the library. One year I checked out a large variety of nonfiction books to share with the students. They loved the books and wanted to check them out immediately. I was so thrilled about their enthusiasm that I let them take the books without keeping an accurate checkout record. The amount of fees I ended up paying for lost books was more than it would have cost to purchase them.

Book Drives

You can also hold a book drive at your school to get more books into classroom libraries. Ask students to donate books that they can bring from home. If your students do not have many books in their homes, encourage them to ask relatives, friends, and neighbors. You can get a large number of books this way, but you may not get the quality or variety you need. You may want to take any inappropriate books that are donated and trade them in at used bookstores.

Garage Sales

Garage sales are another good source for books. Check around your area for dates and times. Some garage sale ads will specify the types of items to be sold. One year, a group of teachers met at a different location monthly for breakfast and book talks. After breakfast, they scoured the surrounding neighborhoods for garage sales and used bookstores in search of good classroom materials.

Borrow and Rotate

Many teachers use their own money or the school's money to build terrific classroom libraries. Sometimes each teacher is allotted an amount specifically for the purchase of books. Check with other teachers at your school to see if they would be willing to lend you some of their books. Or, set up a rotation schedule so everyone can benefit from everyone else's books. The more books the students are exposed to, the better readers they will become.

Grants

If you are really serious about getting books in your classroom, and you need a lot of money to get started (or to maintain), you should stay current on available grants. Apply for any that you come across. Usually, improving literacy is a top priority so you have a good chance of your grant being awarded. Make sure that you are as specific as possible when asking for grant money, and that you portray a clear picture of how badly the books are needed. PTA, Rotary Clubs, local businesses, and national retail stores are all good sources. Don't be afraid to be creative with your request. During both my second and fourth years of teaching (in two different states) I was awarded a Rotary Club grant of $250. I used the money to take two students from each class on a bookstore field trip. The class representatives wrote and delivered speeches on why they should go. They then took orders from their classmates, found the books in the store, and figured the total price as we shopped.

Apply for grants to help purchase classroom library books. Here is the application for the grant I was awarded from the Rotary Club after implementing a schoolwide SSL class.

Teaching Tip

The Lawndale Rotary Club
Lawndale, California
Teacher Mini-Grant
Application

Grant Proposal

I would like to purchase more books for my classroom library. As the reading specialist at Rogers Middle School, I am responsible for helping the children who have reading problems, as well as leading the staff in professional development (in regard to literacy strategies). I am also the person in charge of SSL, our newly implemented schoolwide reading program.

Last year, we started a program called SSL (Supporting Student Literacy). It was a newer version of the existing sustained silent reading program. Changes to the program included: adding writing and read-aloud elements, moving the time of day to before lunch, and requiring folders with reading and writing logs (to increase student accountability). Although we have had some trial-and-error periods and we continue to reflect on what works best, we now have what we consider a strong schoolwide reading program. We still, however, need MORE books!

Every student and staff member at our school participates in SSL class. It is third period every day, and lasts for twenty minutes. Three days a week are devoted to (silent sustained) reading, one day a week is a writing day, and one day a week is a read-aloud day. These three elements are crucial in creating a balanced literacy program. Our goal is to raise the interest level, motivation, and enjoyment of our students in regard to reading, writing, and communicating effectively.

Students change classes for SSL, and therefore every teacher is responsible for "teaching" it. The most important thing that teachers can do is to provide a good model for reading, writing, and speaking. It is also essential that we maintain a large and varied classroom library, and that we can recommend books that would be a good fit with the student(s).

At any grade level, it is important to find books that students will enjoy. The goal is to make them WANT to read. Most of the time, this involves knowing your students and finding out what their likes, dislikes, and interests are.

At the middle school level, this is especially difficult. As these pre-teens go through changes, so do their interests and attitudes. It is vital that we provide high-interest reading material. The books need to be on subjects that are relevant to their lives. As this changes daily, we must continually add to our collection of reading materials.

Materials

I would like to buy more adolescent literature, magazine subscriptions, picture books, and nonfiction. I would also like to purchase more current titles. (Harry Potter and Chicken Soup for the Soul are great examples of series in demand right now!)

I would spend the $250.00 on books that my students suggest. I would concentrate on the above types of literature, because that is where my collection is sparse.

We have a lot of "book talks" and "guest readers" at our school. We are constantly hearing new titles that interest the students. We just do not always have the funds to keep purchasing all of the great books we hear about. This grant would allow me to update my library with current material.

Conclusion

I am involved in all aspects of the improvement of literacy here at Rogers. If I am awarded this grant, and am able to increase my classroom library, it would reach a very large number of students. Not only would my language arts students benefit from access to a larger classroom library, but also my SSL class, and all of the students involved in our after-school programs. Because we have such a huge range of reading levels and students who speak various languages (other than English), we are constantly striving to introduce students to that one book—that "hook"—that will turn them into lifelong readers.

Partners in Education

Some schools are paired with local businesses to form partners in education. If you have such a program at your school, find out who your partners are and approach them for help. If they cannot donate money, they might be able to hold a book drive with their employees for your benefit. If your school does not have any partners in education, why not approach some businesses about becoming partners? This is also a great way to link your school to your community. More often than not, the businesses will send employees to be guest speakers, readers, or helpers in your classroom.

Conferences

Another good way to find great books at discount prices is by going to professional language arts or reading conferences. Not only is this beneficial for your professional development, but it can also help you build your classroom library. I once attended a conference sponsored by the International Reading Association in Orlando, Florida. I was able to hear phenomenal speakers, learn new literacy strategies, talk with authors of young adult literature, meet other teachers, and purchase a variety of books at very low prices. By chance, I found Scholastic's booth at the exact time they were offering copies of *Freak the Mighty* for a dollar each! I picked up a class set immediately. Not only that, but Rodman Philbrick himself was there to autograph the books, and I was given two free passes to attend a sneak preview of the movie version, *The Mighty,* nearly one year ahead of its scheduled release.

Although you might not be that fortunate at every conference, there are some tremendous deals to be found if you are in the market for books.

Bookstores

Advising you to go to a bookstore to find books may sound like common sense, but I am suggesting that you go to any and every bookstore you ever come across. Not all bookstores are alike, and you never know what might be on sale at each. My summer job each year is to help my graduate professor by acting as a facilitating teacher for the workshops she gives for other educators in various cities all over the United States. A group of us live and work together with her each summer, teaching and learning from others all over the nation. No matter where we are, how much time we have, or how little sleep we've gotten, we always hit the bookstores in these areas. The section for bargain books is a particular favorite of mine. I will never forget the time my friend Lee found a hardback copy of Paul Jennings's *Uncovered! Weird, Weird Stories* for $1.99. I had been diligently searching everywhere in my hometown for that book after I heard his hilarious story "A Mouthful." It was on back order and would not be available in my town for quite some time. You can imagine how green I was with envy.

Just a few summers ago, I was looking for *Harry Potter and the Goblet of Fire.* It had just been released, and, having read the first three books in the series, I wanted to read the fourth one as soon as I possibly could. I had been too busy during the school year to remember to put my name on a list to get it, so I thought I would have to wait for months. I was on a trip with some friends in Key West, Florida. As we were driving back to Orlando, we decided to stop at a trucker's rest stop to get some water. Guess what I found in the gift section of their coffee shop? I bought the last copy of *Harry Potter and the Goblet of Fire* the day after it was released! I was thrilled with my find at this roadside bookstore. You never know what you might find in the most unexpected places. So if you happen across an interesting bookstore, stop and take a look.

Book Club Points

Several companies send brochures advertising book clubs for kids. I love using Scholastic's Tab and Arrow brochures. Not only do they have a lot of supplemental material for each content area, and current young adult titles, but they also offer bonus points. If you order yourself, or if you have students who like to order, you can earn enough bonus points to get free books. I recently ordered a class set of Jerry Spinelli's *Maniac Magee* and paid absolutely nothing. Every month they offer new books for students and resource books for teachers. They have a "buy five books, get the sixth book free" promotion monthly, and they ship within two weeks. If you have the time to pass the brochures out to students, or even if you occasionally order yourself, it is well worth it.

Books to Hook the Reader: Knowing Your Students

I'm looking forward to the fall. I know I'll be surprised, perplexed, and interested; I know I'll learn. And I know, finally, that what I can take to heart about eighth graders is how they wear their hearts on their sleeves. They can be highly emotional—elated, confused, angry, afraid—but their high emotions are usually short-lived. Water flows over the dam in torrents in my classroom because I'm learning what to take seriously and seriously respond to, and what to wait out.
Nancie Atwell, *In the Middle*

It isn't enough to have a wealth of books; you need to make sure you have the right books. How do you know which books will hook the students in your classroom? The best way, as I have said before, is by getting to know your students.

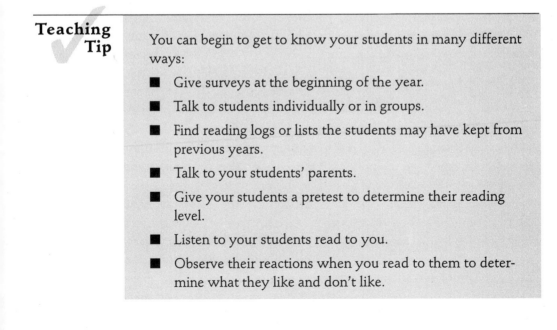

Teaching Tip

You can begin to get to know your students in many different ways:

- Give surveys at the beginning of the year.
- Talk to students individually or in groups.
- Find reading logs or lists the students may have kept from previous years.
- Talk to your students' parents.
- Give your students a pretest to determine their reading level.
- Listen to your students read to you.
- Observe their reactions when you read to them to determine what they like and don't like.

■ Check their cumulative folder to check for pertinent information.

■ Talk to school counselors or previous teachers who might know the students well.

■ Check their standardized test scores to see what areas they are strong in, and where they might struggle.

■ Consider giving a survey to measure multiple intelligences, so you'll know what kind of learner the student is.

You can read young adult literature ad nauseam, but if you don't know what your students like, you won't be able to match them with appropriate books. Find out their interests before you give book talks, before you choose what to read aloud for the week. We know that to hook our students books must have charm, magic, impact, and appeal. Are you offering books that have these qualities? Do the stories have meaning and relevance for your particular students?

I once mistakenly recommended *Where the Red Fern Grows* to a small group of sixth-grade students in Florida. Although this is a fantastic story (and a real tearjerker for me) my students that year hated it. The entire time they were reading it, they were asking me questions such as, "Why does he have to walk all the way to the other town? Why doesn't he hitchhike? What kind of dumb dog is a coonhound, anyway? People don't hunt anymore, do they? What kind of names are Dan and Ann? Couldn't he think of anything cooler? He should have saved his money for some real dogs." At the end of the story when Little Ann and Old Dan die, the kids actually laughed and said they knew that would happen. I soon realized that my twentieth-century students could not relate at all to the trials of Billy. Foolishly, I had chosen a novel that once had appeal for me, but did not for these students.

When stocking your shelves with books, make sure you have books of all topics, lengths, and genres. This should include, but not be limited to, picture books, newspapers, magazines, big-print books, classics, young adult literature, sports stories, romances, short stories, and mysteries. You might also consider laminated comic strips, plays, activity books, joke books, or cartoon books (Calvin and Hobbes is still a favorite in my classes). For struggling readers, you might even use laminated copies of student work, student-made picture books, short excerpts from books, poetry collections, nonfiction, and books on tape. Be sure to validate the choices the students make, and know that your "highest reader" will not always choose the most difficult book. I had one student who loved reading the Chicken Soup series. She had read all of the stories in three different books. I noticed that her writing style had become more personal and detailed as she was reading these books. When I checked her reading log, she had not recorded any of the hundred-plus stories she had read. When I asked her why, she answered, "I didn't think they counted."

Teaching Tip

Be sure to include these favorite authors when building your classroom library:

Avi	Hunt, Irene
Cisneros, Sandra	Lowry, Lois
Cooney, Caroline	Myers, Walter Dean
Cormier, Robert	Mazer, Norma Fox
Crutcher, Chris	Paterson, Katherine
Curtis, Christopher Paul	Paulsen, Gary
Dahl, Roald	Peck, Richard
Danziger, Paula	Peck, Robert Newton
Draper, Sharon	Sachar, Louis
Duncan, Lois	Spinelli, Jerry
Gantos, Jack	Stine, R. L.
Hinton, S. E.	Voight, Cynthia

Audiobooks

It is difficult for some teachers to allow students to read all types of reading material during sustained silent reading time. They would prefer that their students read only chapter books, "classics," or core literature. It should be obvious that I advocate the reading of all types of materials. One reason is that SSL should be stress-free time for the students. The students should not feel pressure to read a certain type or level of book. First of all, the material they read should be of their choosing. More important, they may choose to read a magazine or a picture book because it is the only material they can actually comprehend if they are reading independently. Other lower-level readers may have trouble choosing anything at all because they don't find the books on their reading level appealing. How do we support all students and ensure they have access to materials they will find challenging and enjoyable? I believe audiobooks fill these needs perfectly.

In *The Foundations of Literacy,* Don Holdaway writes, "We gain much greater control over repetitions when we bring a listening-post into the room. The less ready children are then able to gain much more massive repetition before 'reading' than they otherwise would. The tape recorder seems to be the second most important invention for literacy after the book" (1979, p. 73). Allowing students to listen to audiobooks while following along with an exact copy of the text is almost like having shared reading, described by Margaret Mooney as "eyes past print with voice support," without the teacher. The student sees the words (eyes past print) at the exact time they hear them (voice support). It allows many students to have higher-level reading experiences with their own text, independently. It gives lower-level readers the ability to read, enjoy, and understand a story that would otherwise be too difficult for them. Make certain that the book exactly matches the tape. Often the tape is an abridged version and the book is not, or vice versa. Buy the unabridged version of the book on tape so the students' texts will match verbatim.

Audiobooks can be expensive, so again, look for them to go on sale. It used to be that you had to order them from a catalog and could never find them in a store. Now, many main bookstores such as Barnes & Noble and Borders sell books on tape right in the store. If you do prefer to shop by catalog or via the Internet, a great source is Recorded Books, Inc. These titles are all unabridged, are of good quality, can easily be exchanged, and ship in a reasonable amount of time. Other options are to check them out from your local library (knowing, though, that you will be able to use them only for a short amount of time), borrowing from other teachers, or checking to see if any stores near you specialize in books on tape. In Torrance, California, a store called Audiobooks allows you to check out or purchase books on tape. They will also order tapes for you if they do not have what you want in stock.

Some students won't want to use audiobooks because they are afraid it looks as though they can't read or because it "isn't cool." To combat those feelings, try modeling this activity by listening to a book on tape yourself during class. If you really use books on tape, you might mention to the class how much you enjoy listening to them. Explain to the students that many people (even adults) listen to audiobooks because they still actually enjoy hearing stories out loud. Clarify that there are other reasons to listen to these tapes: long car rides, commutes, or just because people lead busy lives and like to hear stories while they drive, jog, or bike.

You might want to have a week where you ask students to rotate and each take a turn listening to a book on tape. (You could do the same for a picture book or any other material that might have a stigma associated with it.)

The Logistics of Using Audiobooks

If you do encourage your students to use audiobooks, there are some specifics you should know for easy implementation. First, you should buy a portable cassette player. Do not use the traditional large single recorders you can check out from your library, that you have to plug into the wall. This will severely inhibit your students' mobility and cause more distractions during SSR. I also suggest that you not buy cassette players with radios. This may sound silly, but it is sensible advice. I made the mistake of bringing in my own portable cassette recorder for students to use, and it happened to have a radio with it. I soon found out that a student was not listening to the book on tape when I heard the heavy beat of rap music reverberating from his corner of the room. Be careful, even if you do purchase cassette players without radios. I had another student who sneaked his own country music into the player while, ironically, pretending to read Cynthia DeFelice's book *Weasel.* He was found out because I noticed his head bobbing in a peculiar way, and it wasn't to the beat of his pages turning.

You also want to devise some sort of system for using audio-books. Either purchase multiple copies of the same book and color-code them for checkout, or let only one student read a particular book at one time. When many students listen to the same tape and stop at different places, the next student has a hard time finding his or her place again.

Storage

Storing the tapes, cassette players, and headphones is also an issue. I always hang the headphones to preserve the wires and foam ear-pieces longer. I found that when the wires are wrapped around the headphones, they tend to split and the foam earpieces sometimes tear. If you put nails in the wall, or perhaps a hook that has adhesive, the headphones hang easily.

Teaching Tip

One good place to hang these is behind a bookcase. If you place the headphones on the nail or hook, and let the wires hang straight down (behind the bookcase), you will have minimum damage.

Place the audiobooks next to the corresponding book prominently displayed on an accessible bookshelf.

If you need to, be aware that the foam earpieces on some headphones can be detached, washed, and reused. I have also found that some electronics stores sell the foam pieces separately, if yours need to be replaced.

It is also important to store each audiobook next to the corresponding book. This allows students to easily find the materials they need to get started.

If you think it is necessary to have cassette players out of students' reach until they are ready to use them, you could store them in a locked cabinet. If you choose this option, keep in mind that *you* are the one who will have to constantly go to the locked cabinet to retrieve them, which can be quite inconvenient. (They will be used all the time!)

Batteries

Where to store the batteries will also be an individual decision. Most cassette players require two double-A batteries. In my classes, tape players were often inadvertently left in the "play" position. This quickly runs down the battery. Some years, my batteries have tended to disappear after only one use. I have always been able to keep my cassette players out in the open, but I require students to check batteries in and out through me each time they are used. You could also assign this duty to a responsible student.

Another option is to buy rechargeable batteries and a battery charger. It is simple enough to charge the batteries each night when they are not in use. An easy way to manage this is to assign a student in your last-period class to be in charge of collecting the batteries and placing them in the charger. In the morning, a student in your first-period class can retrieve the batteries from the charger and distribute them. Although buying a charger and rechargeable batteries is more expensive, it may be worth it if you plan to use them frequently.

Purchasing Cassette Players

Some people advocate buying top-quality players so they will last through more than one class. I have had the same cassette recorders for four years now and they are still functioning beautifully. The amount you spend on them will depend on how delicately you think your students will handle them, and how long you think they will last. Two places that sell cassette players with headphones (but without radios) relatively inexpensively are Target and Radio Shack.

Remember that you will eventually wean your students off using audiobooks, once they have the capacity to be independent readers.

Readability

You also need to make sure you have books of many different readability levels. There are many approaches to finding the reading levels of your students. You can rely on test scores (state standardized or district approved) and fluency tests, or you may want to ask the reading specialist at your school to help you better assess your students. I use the Degrees of Reading Power (DRP) test to measure reading comprehension as a pretest and posttest each year. The DRP test is published by Touchstone Applied Science Applications (TASA). They have a CD called *DRP Booklinks* that will tell you the DRP level of a novel. To find the readability level of a textbook, go to their Web site (www.tasaliteracy.com). If your textbook is not listed, you can send them the book and they will analyze it free of charge. Once you have their DRP levels, you can match these with your students' scores. If you are interested in finding more ways to estimate the difficulty of texts, I highly recommend Chapter 3 of Richard Allington's book *What Really Matters for Struggling Readers* (2001). It contains an entire section called "Methods for Estimating Text Complexity" that is fantastic.

It is also wise to check book jackets. Many books have the interest level and the reading level clearly marked on the back cover. Keep in mind that no readability level is completely accurate. You must consider the whole picture. Your knowledge of the interests, motivation, and abilities of your particular students and the subject and difficulty of the text in question will give you more insight than any readability score.

Student-Selected Reading

*A classic—something that everybody wants to have read and
nobody wants to read.*
Mark Twain, *Mark Twain's Speeches* (Paine)

Finally, you must allow the students to choose what they want to
read. This means that they can read books, magazines, short stories, comic books, or anything else that looks good to them. It
needs to be okay for them to switch books if they have one they
don't like, or abandon a book without finishing it. They need to
know that that is acceptable. Too many times teachers try to assign
books for SSR. I realize that teachers have a lot of material to cover
and that sometimes SSR looks like the perfect place to stick that
material you are afraid you won't get through, but please, don't do
it! This jeopardizes the very nature of sustained silent reading, and
it breaks the trust you have been building to make your class a
reading community. I knew a teacher who insisted that his students create book reports for each SSR book they finished. Can you
imagine writing a report for every bit of personal reading you do? It
would probably make you stop reading altogether. In many cases,
that is exactly what happens. In this instance, it only made the students pretend to read the same book for an extraordinarily long
time. They knew this would allow them to complete only a minimum number of book reports. Filling this reading time with assignments, or forcing certain books will not work. It is the true antithe-
sis of "free reading."

Classroom Environment

Building a successful SSR program includes creating an environment
conducive to reading, writing, thinking, and learning. With any classroom situation, students need to feel comfortable and safe, both
mentally and physically. Think about your own reading preferences
when designing the layout of your classroom. If you are reading this
book, you are probably an avid reader yourself. Where do you prefer
to read? How are you reading this book right now? I would guess

that most of you spend time reading for pleasure in comfortable places and positions, such as resting in a comfortable chair, lounging in a recliner, curled up on the couch, tucked under the covers in bed, or even relaxing with your favorite blanket or pillow on the floor. Some of you may prefer soft lighting, some may prefer bright. You may get pleasure from reading outside, whereas others like to remain indoors. Although it is unlikely that we can please and accommodate every single reader in our classroom, we should be able to offer a multitude of choices. Pillows, blankets, beanbags, throw rugs, and comfortable chairs or couches can be positioned together to create an inviting reading atmosphere. Before I constructed my reading corner, I had students read at their desks. I had a student ask if she could stretch out on the floor during SSR instead. To me, the thought was rather repulsive. The carpet was somewhat old; it was thin, making the surface hard; there was a multitude of unidentified stains; and it was in desperate need of replacing. I reluctantly acquiesced, though, and was delighted that I decided to grant her request. She was so thrilled to be out of that desk that she didn't stop smiling the entire period. Not only that, but she read more pages that day and was more focused than ever before. Other students, of course, followed her lead and asked if they, too, could read somewhere other than their desk. Before long, more than half the class was out of their seats and all over the floor. This may sound out of control to some teachers, but the bottom line is, they were all reading.

For my reading corner, I bought two beanbags from a local department store (I found durable denim ones that have lasted three years at JCPenney for $35 each), and an old love seat ($10) from a garage sale. Another teacher donated a throw rug. I also pleaded with the librarian to donate a circular bookrack, and she graciously agreed. I placed the throw rug on the floor in the middle and had books out and open along the tops of the shelves.

I set up a reading area in a corner of my room. I had two old bookcases that I placed in parallel positions along two walls, framing the area I had set up for reading.

Teaching Tip

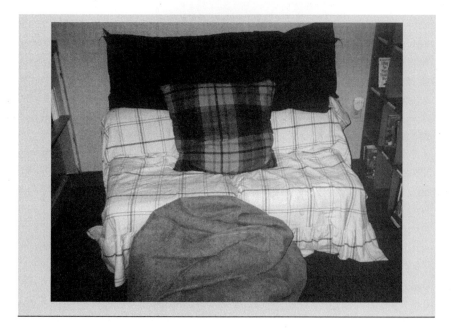

Organization

Once you have a lot of books, you will want to consider organizing and displaying them so they are easily accessible. One of my bookcases was actually used previously for storing backpacks during physical education classes. Rather than traditional long shelves, this bookcase had small square cubbyholes. I decided these spaces would be perfect for organizing the books. I taught my students (through a mini-lesson) different genres, and had them sort the books by genres and label the cubbyholes accordingly.

I also placed the more popular books and big oversized books open on top of the bookcase for easy viewing.

Another idea I like, if you don't have enough shelves, is to purchase rain gutters from hardware or home improvement stores. These can be nailed to the walls and used as ready-made bookshelves.

If you are using some sort of record-keeping device, such as a reading log or reading list, it is important to also have these stored in convenient places so students can obtain them easily after reading.

In setting up your classroom and in creating a safe environment, make sure you include the students in the decision-making process. Remember that it is their classroom, too, and that you want them to have ownership of many aspects of it.

CHAPTER FOUR

The Teacher's Role: Leading and Assessing SSL

In my life I had just two teachers who invited me to become a reader. Two was enough. . . . Time and choice are important, but for these kids the teacher's individual responses to them, their tastes, and their troubles will be another key.

Nancie Atwell, *Side by Side*

I believe that the way you address your students and interact with them on a daily basis is an excellent predictor of how successful your SSL program, or any other learning experience, will be. In *What Matters Most for Struggling Readers,* Allington finds from reading the many studies on the effect of high-quality teaching that "nothing is as powerful as the quality of the teacher in predicting the achievement of children. Neither parents nor socioeconomic status of the family were as powerful as good instruction in shaping the academic futures of students" (2001).

So what does it take to be a high-quality teacher of an SSL program? You must take on the roles of researcher, facilitator, listener, questioner, motivator, and most important, reader. You research to uncover your students' interests. You facilitate the time period by teaching them the daily routine, helping them choose books, ensuring the noise level is conducive to reading, and monitoring behavior. Be attentive even to minor logistical problems such as which students get to sit in the beanbag chair or listen to the audiobooks that day. You need to constantly listen to your students when they talk about themselves or about books, and respond to their questions.

You should also question their choices, thoughts, and reasoning while you check for understanding. Support them in their quest to become independent readers, offer individual attention, reinforce reading strategies, and motivate them to want to read more and learn more. Eleanor Duckworth, in her book *The Having of Wonderful Ideas and Other Essays on Teaching and Learning,* defines our role in this way: "By 'teacher,' I mean someone who engages learners, who seeks to involve each person wholly—mind, sense of self, sense of humor, range of interests, interactions with other people—in learning" (1996).

Finally, model positive reading behaviors by reading as much as you possibly can. If students see that you value reading, that it is something you legitimately find enjoyable, they will begin to appreciate reading, too.

I said in my introduction that you don't have to be a "reading" teacher to make SSR work. You don't, but I do believe you have to be an avid reader. You should be reading books for pleasure, but also professional books. How else will you know about the latest research? Jim Trelease in *The Read-Aloud Handbook* writes about how seldom teachers are seen reading and how great it would be if they could give book talks to their students about classroom library books they actually read. He found that the

> harsh reality is most teachers don't read much. One study of 224 teachers pursuing graduate degrees showed that teachers read few or no professional journals that included research. More than half said they had read only one or two professional books in the previous year, and an additional 20 percent said they had read nothing in the last six months or one year. What did they read beyond professional material?
> - 22 percent read a newspaper only once a week.
> - 75 percent were only "light" book readers—one or two a year.
> - 25 percent were "heavy" book readers (three to four books in a month). This means that teachers don't read any more often than adults in the general population. (2001)

I believe you should think of your classroom as a giant book club. If you have ever been a part of a successful book club, you already know the key elements. The best book clubs are filled with people who love to read, people who get excited about a story, who cry over a poem, who laugh out loud when reading. These people love to share books, hate it when the story is over, and run out to buy copies for all their friends. They ask questions of themselves, they question the other members, and they can't wait to talk about the books, sometimes to whoever might be willing to listen. You should strive to bring your classroom to this level.

Teaching Tip

Start a book club at your school for staff or for students. Below is a sample book club invitation form.

You Are Invited . . .
You are cordially invited to join the first young adult book club! Because there are so many great young adult novels, and so many of our students are NOT avid readers, I thought it might be fun to read young adult literature. That would

enable us to recommend more books to our students AND we would be able to discuss these books with them intelligently. I actually really enjoy many of these books, and I hope you will, too!

If you are interested in choosing and reading books, and you like to meet (and eat?) to discuss them, then this club is for you! Young adult books often take adults only a week or so to read—so if you think you might not have time to participate, that may not be the case. We would meet once a month, at the most. Once we find out how many teachers are interested, and what grade level they teach, we could plan to meet during lunch, before or after school, or in the evenings (for dinner?). I am open to all suggestions and would love to start arming teachers with material to entice students into reading!

Please fill out the bottom portion of this form if you are interested in participating. Simply place it in my mailbox by Wednesday. If I get (any) responses, we can meet to select our first book. I have a million book lists we can plow through, and/or we can use teacher recommendations. (I know many of us heard some great excerpts last week during Read Across America that we now want to read.)

Thanks and keep reading!

Name: _____ Prep Period: _____ Grade: _____

Subject: _____

____ I would love to be in a book club. Sign me up!

____ I don't have time now. Ask me again (when you're on the second book).

____ Thank you, but I am not interested.

Last, remember that your students will not all be in the same place in regard to their progress as readers. You need to evaluate them over time to see their improvements, rather than compare them with each other.

Lead and Read

Children who haven't heard words sing, who have not experienced
words that make them laugh and cry, words that make them go
suddenly quiet, even pensive, are not going to be readers, no matter
how adept they are at decoding.
Susan Ohanian, *One Size Fits Few*

The best way to make books come alive in your room is to lead your students to books. The best way to accomplish that is to read to them and read with them. Leading your students to books means that you are informed enough to know what is out there and what matches your students' interests. It means that you have read a variety of books on a multitude of topics that you can honestly recommend. You need to stay updated so you know what titles and authors are popular and current. Sometimes you can entice them simply by reading excerpts of a great story to the entire class, or by quietly handing a certain student a book you know he or she will find special. Other times, you might have to keep searching for the perfect suggestion for that hard-to-please reader. M. J. was a student of mine in Florida during my first year of teaching. He had just read a complete book on his own for the first time—one of the titles in the Goosebumps series by R. L. Stine. When he finished it, he showed me the inside jacket of the book where other Goosebumps titles were listed. He pointed to *The Cuckoo Clock of Doom* and said, "I HAVE to read this book. Can we please get it for the classroom? I really want to read it next." Because I was so impressed with his enthusiasm, I went to the store and purchased it that day. I wrote his name on it and gave it to him privately the next morning. I told him it was a gift from me to him; it was his to read and take home. He jumped up and literally screamed. Then he yelled, "I own a book! I own a book!"

When recommending books, you definitely have to know the difference between suggesting and forcing. Some students won't want unsolicited suggestions from you. You have to wait until these students look stuck, or until they actually ask for help. Reading young adult books is the best preparation. My students are always amazed when I can talk with them about a book they are reading, or when they see me reading what they consider "their type of book." You are much more credible if you are recommending books you really have read. It is especially useful to know the plot when a student is trying to pull one over on you by making up a summary, pretending to have read the book. I want to be clear that I am not suggesting you read books that don't interest you—students will see through that. Choose young adult books on topics that naturally, sincerely appeal to you. You might be surprised at the common interests you share with the teens in your class, and what doors might open as a result.

Accountability

Some followers of SSR programs will argue that there should not be any accountability; that it takes the fun out of reading for students. I believe that my students needed the accountability piece (they actually asked for it) and it worked for us. Some classes may not need to have any type of log or grading system—but mine did.

My students kept portfolios. We decided they would keep a section in their portfolio titled SSL. This section would contain a reading log and a writing log. I could not find very many logs already in print that I liked, so as a class, we made our own. These were really simple versions that suited our needs perfectly (I used the logs shown in Appendix 1). The purpose of the reading log was to document the dates of each reading session, the titles and pages read each day, and a brief written response by the student. The purpose of the writing log was to record topics or titles students wrote about each day. Students would not be responsible for documenting what was read to them on read-aloud days (Fridays). Points would be given to students simply for turning in completed reading and writing logs. This was intentionally a simple task. I wanted the information they were supplying to be for their own record keeping—so we could track their progress. These logs later became an excellent tool for parent conferences and for placing students in language arts classes in subsequent years.

It should be obvious that I believe in a student-centered curriculum. My students make decisions on a daily basis in my classroom, and often vote on novels or lessons we are reading or working on. Students often help me create rubrics for assignments and therefore have an understanding of what they can accomplish. They know what is expected of them, and they know what excellent work looks like. I use portfolios as a tool for assessment, and my students are accustomed to using them to lead conferences with their parents each trimester. Previously, before the start of SSL, I had not carried this "student-driven" philosophy into the planning and grading of sustained silent reading. I thought that not including them in that process was a mistake; a mistake that, more than likely, contributed to the failure of that program. Consequently, I asked for their input when creating a grading system for SSL.

To Grade or Not to Grade?

The outrage over students reading for points instead of pleasure is
a false alarm. If you surveyed human beings on the reasons for
reading, the answers would include: money; competitiveness;
grades; degrees/diplomas; escape; curiosity; filling time; pleasure;
and enrichment of the spirit—depending on the person's
circumstances on a given day.
There are many books and articles I read only because they are
associated with my job; many are boring, but as an educator and
author I read them to stay abreast professionally. Wouldn't this be
considered reading for money? I hope my physician does the same.
Most of the books college students read in school aren't for intrinsic
reasons—and we all know it. How different is that from reading
for points?
Jim Trelease, *The Read-Aloud Handbook*

As I said earlier, the original sustained silent reading programs, in their unaltered forms, had specific guidelines saying there would be no reports, questions, or records kept—thus, no accountability. I believe this method can work, but it did not work with my struggling, at-risk, middle school students. Each class of students is unique, and what the members of that class can and are willing to do is also distinct. I believe that every teacher should study his or her particular class before deciding whether to grade a silent reading period and how to do it. In this chapter, I am simply sharing what worked with my students.

The very fact that my students asked for a point system was reason enough for me to help them create one. In the words of Jim Trelease, "If grownups can have their frequent flyer and traveler points, why can't the kids accumulate their reading points? Furthermore, isn't the report card the original 'point' program?" (2001).

I wasn't actually giving points for the number of books read, but for participating in the program each day. I asked my students each to write down the number of points they thought each day should be worth. The answers ranged from 1 to 100. Initially I thought they were trying to be funny, but after discussing it with them, I realized that they all just had very different views on how much they wanted SSL to count. I then reminded them of the other things we do that earn points so they could make a comparison. With a little prodding from me, we decided that the reading and writing logs would be worth ten points each. Students could earn points by simply completing the logs daily and turning them in at the end of the week. Each log would be worth ten points, five points for each entry. Thus, if a student earned all points possible, their grade would be as such:

Monday: SSR log complete: 5 points

Tuesday: SSW log complete (title listed): 5 points

Wednesday: SSR log complete: 5 points

Thursday: SSW log complete (title listed): 5 points

Friday: no log necessary: Points N/A

Total Weekly Points (both logs combined): 20 points

These points were then recorded in my grade book on a weekly basis. Each Friday, students came in and listened to the selection that was read to them. At the conclusion of the reading, they got their portfolios and opened them to the SSL section. I would walk around the room and check for complete entries. (I did not read each entry in its entirety, but instead checked for the mere presence of an entry.) The points for the logs were added and averaged with other assignments: class assignments (usually worth 10 points each for a total of 50 points a week), homework (usually worth 10 points each week), and test grades (50–100 points once or twice each trimester). These scores were added together to compute a final report-card grade. For each trimester, SSL points were usually worth approximately 20 percent of the overall language arts grade.

The students helped determine how many points each entry would be worth. I reminded them of our other assignments and made sure they were aware of how much weight this SSL grade would carry in determining their grade in the class. No one complained on Fridays when I checked logs, because everyone had had a part in determining the grading process.

Again, how much you want SSR to count in your class, or whether you choose to grade it at all, is up to you. Find out what works for your students and put it into practice. Just make sure your expectations are clear to the students from the beginning.

Reflect, Revise, and Analyze

Perhaps this is the way to teach children. First, we must love music or literature or math . . . so much that we cannot stand to keep that love to ourselves. Then, with energy and enthusiasm and enormous respect for the learner, we share our love. . . . And we don't give out love in little pieces, we give it full and running over. We don't edit or censor or predigest; we entrust in its fullness to someone we hope will love it too.

Katherine Paterson, *The Spying Heart*

After almost six months of the new SSL program, I started interviewing students individually and documenting their thoughts and opinions about it. I first asked, "How do you feel about our SSL program and the changes we made?" Some of the responses are as follows:

> I love it. I am so glad we made the changes. I really enjoy the part where I can ask for help when I choose a book and I like the writing days, too. I feel like we have more freedom than before, even though we now fill out logs. I really don't think it's that hard, but before I did.
> *Amber, seventh grader*

> It's okay. It is definitely better than it was. I now feel like I know what I am supposed to be doing. Before, I just sort of pretended.
> *David, seventh grader*

> I love the SSW days. It's like I get to write notes to my friends twice a week. I hope you are not reading them. It's fun and much better than five days of reading.
> *Charlene, seventh grader*

> I think we needed the changes. It was real boring reading all five days, even when I had a book I liked. I like doing different things on different days, but I like Fridays the best. I actually enjoy being read to, and I didn't think I would.
> *Michael, eighth grader*

> I sort of liked the program better the way it was before. I liked that we didn't have to write before and didn't have to keep any logs. I don't like the writing days we have now. I never feel like I have anything to say. It is hard for me to fill up the time by just writing. I do like the days when you read to us, though. I don't always like it when students read to us on those days. Overall, the new program is okay.
> *Sara, eighth grader*

> I like it okay except for the writing days. I just can't think of what to write about. I spend half of the time worrying because I

can't come up with a good subject. I would prefer to have more read-aloud days and less writing days.
Frank, eighth grader

I feel good about SSL. I like that we helped make it. It is much better than before because now you let us talk more about the books, and you are there to talk to us instead of just reading your own book all the time.
Lisa, sixth grader

I don't like it quite as much as what we did before. I feel like you are watching us more now and expecting us to tell you a lot about the books we read. I feel a little more tired because you want us to share so much.
Jonathan, sixth grader

I only like the read-aloud days. Those are the only days I really enjoy. I would like to have five days of reading aloud instead of the way it is now.
Joey, sixth grader

My observations were as follows:

■ Most students shared positive feelings about the new program, with only minor complaints. I think it is important to note that those students who did complain later offered suggestions on how to make things better. I don't think they would have voluntarily done that had they not felt ownership of SSL.

■ Students *were* reading more. The fact that they had to write down the number of pages they read on each SSR day seemed to make them stick with one book longer than they had previously.

■ More students were volunteering to read on Fridays. A drawback to this is that the "audience" sometimes became disinterested if I wasn't the one reading.

■ Students were eager to show the SSL section of their portfolio to other classmates, teachers, and parents. It seemed to be a section they were proud of.

- Students consistently earned more points for SSL than any other class assignment.

- Students were not sharing on writing days. The same students were volunteering each week.

- It took a long time for students to get settled into writing on Tuesdays and Thursdays, and many students were writing only a paragraph or so in the twenty-minute period.

Although I was helping students select books and having conferences with the students on SSR days, I still managed to model SSR by reading young adult literature myself. I was also continually encouraging students to share their own book recommendations. I can honestly say that I modeled writing on every single SSW day. I wanted the students to know that I valued this time, too. Students entered the room early, and often were eager to share their latest book with me. They did not try to pack up their belongings early, but instead kept reading until I said it was time to stop.

I continued to talk to students frequently about the class, asking for their opinions and suggestions. Overwhelmingly, the students asked for more read-aloud days. Often on Mondays, they would ask me to continue reading what I had been reading on Friday. They were also rapidly checking out the books that I was reading and recommending. In addition, these books were getting returned at a quicker pace, and students were talking to me about the stories (so I know they were really reading them). Furthermore, students from other classes came to check out books from me. When we celebrated Read Across America (the birthday of Dr. Seuss) with a "read-in," three times the number of students volunteered to be guest readers than the number who had signed up the previous year. I was also told by several students that the library was getting "too crowded for comfort" during lunchtime. This led me to believe that possibly more books were getting checked out. (The list of overdue books was definitely longer than it had been before.)

Student Survey Responses

I again enlisted the help of a survey to get data from my students about the effectiveness of this program. All of the comments shared (orally) from the students were positive, and I genuinely felt that we were becoming a community of readers (see Appendix 2).

As expected, the majority of the students liked read-aloud days the best. Out of 30 randomly chosen surveys, 23 responded that they liked the read-aloud days best, 6 liked reading days best, and 1 liked the writing days best. Most students thought that 15 or 20 minutes was enough time for SSL. When asked about the time currently allotted, 15 students said that what we had was enough time, 6 said it was too much, and 9 thought it was too little. In regard to comprehension, it seems that most students did not realize a significant change. Twenty-five students said, "I don't know" when asked if they understood what they read more now than they did at the beginning of the year, 2 students responded "no," and only 3 wrote "yes."

Most students (22) said their language arts grades changed for the better, but not all grades had been given to the students at the time they were filling out the surveys. More than half (23) of the students wrote that they were reading more than they had before this year of SSL, and 10 said they were writing more. In response to whether they enjoyed reading and writing more now, the majority of students said they did. Twenty-two responded that they enjoyed reading more than before, and 17 liked writing more. Twenty-six students wanted to see SSL continue the next year, but very few students wrote comments explaining why, or what they would change.

It is clear to me that the positive classroom attitudes and behaviors I was observing were consistent with survey results. Students were enthusiastic about SSL and were at least willing to explore how they could improve in reading and writing. I was encouraged and excited by their responses.

Improvements

Although the survey results were promising, I still thought we could improve the program. I had three major concerns:

1. It was fantastic that students were now really reading, but I was worried about running out of materials (money) to keep my classroom library updated.

2. It was difficult to get students to share their reading and writing at the end of each SSL period.

3. It was even more difficult to get the students to actually focus enough to write on the SSW days.

To address those problems, I examined what was working and added to it. I will outline the key points that I believe make SSL, or any reading program, a success.

Allowing for Talk

It was a new year and I was again explaining to my class of seventh-grade students the difference between a reluctant reader and a struggling reader. I told them that they might actually be able to read something, but be reluctant to—they find it boring or dull. I told them that if they are a struggling reader, they are having trouble actually reading it—it is too difficult, or there is vocabulary that is above their comprehension and or decoding skills. So I wanted them to tell me, as they came up for personal conferences, where and when during the school day they felt like a struggling reader, and where and when they felt reluctant.

I placed two books on my desk for the purpose of discussion. One was our shared reading book; the other was a textbook. A student came up for her conference. When she sat down, I asked her to talk to me about what kind of reader she was during the school day. She pointed to the shared reading book.

"When we read that, I feel ructant—real ructant," she said.

"You feel RE-luctant?" I enunciated. "Why?"

"Well, I don't like that book as much as the other books we've read. It is getting boring," she explained.

"Okay, what about when you read this kind of book?" I asked, pointing to the textbook.

No response.

"How do you feel about this book, the textbook?" I asked. She shrugged her shoulders.

"Is it hard for you? Can you read this book or is it too hard?" I asked.

Again, she shrugged her shoulders. I said her name in a questioning tone.

"I'm shrugging, I'm shruggin'!" she exclaimed. "You asked me if I am ructant or shruggin'—I'm shrugging!"

When you start your SSL program, make sure the students know you expect them to talk. I never would have learned how this student felt about herself as a reader if I had not had that conference with her. Silent reading no longer has to be silent the entire time—it really shouldn't be. If you set the example by walking around and talking to students about their books, asking them about how they chose their book, and sharing what you are reading, they will soon follow your lead.

Encourage talk during SSR as well as during the sharing time at the conclusion of it. So many students are used to being yelled at for talking during a silent reading period, it might take them a while to realize that occasional talking is acceptable. If you see a student whispering to another, and you are certain they are talking about what they are reading, allow it. Your goal should be for your students to be excited about what they are reading, and if they are showing their book to another classmate, they must be enjoying it.

However, you need to continue to monitor the noise level in the room. Some students need it to be very quiet, almost silent, to concentrate on reading. Others have a higher tolerance for noise. Observe how your students are handling things, and adjust students' seating, if necessary. More than likely, you will hear from the students themselves if conditions are not to their liking.

To get the students involved in sharing their books at the end of the period, I have started discussing the books I am reading. If I speak first, and talk for just a minute or two, students see that talking about what they are reading is not so difficult, and they start to volunteer themselves. I make sure that I'm sharing a quick response by simply saying the name of my book and how I feel about it, so students know I don't expect them to give a book report. It is also extremely important to be honest about your feelings for the book you are reading. If you are at a point that is hilarious, share it. If you are reading a passage that is confusing, and you've had to read it more than once, admit that. If you had to stop and look up a word in the dictionary, confess that, too. Make sure students know what reading is really like—don't sugarcoat it. Being the teacher does not mean you have to be perfect. The more you can share about your own reading experiences, the more you are teaching them. It also shows them that book talks can be given any time during the reading of a book, not merely at the completion of one. This lets students know that what we are reading and what we have to say about it is of constant importance. It gets them away from the notion of questions at the end and demonstrates that pleasure can be derived periodically throughout a book.

Another good technique is to ask a few students individually at the beginning of the period if they would mind sharing at the end. This allows those students to prepare what they are going to say, rather than being put on the spot. It also guarantees that those selected students will focus even more on what they are reading that day, because they know they will be giving a mini–book talk on their reading material. If you ask someone to volunteer, be willing to accept "no" for an answer. I do not think the book talks can or should be forced.

One last idea for sparking discussions if you are not getting any volunteers is to ask general questions, posed to the whole group.

Teaching Tip

The following are sample questions I have recently used that work well in starting discussions in my class of formerly reluctant sharers:

- Is anyone reading a book by a female/male author?

- Is anyone reading a book with a male/female main character?

- Is anyone reading nonfiction?

- Can anyone share an example of dialog in a book?

- Is anyone reading science fiction? (Any genre would work here.)

- Has anyone learned an interesting fact from the reading?

- Who is reading a book by a teen author?

- Who has a book that takes place in the South?

- Who has a book by a local author?
- Who has a book he/she would like to recommend to others?

Any question that will force students to think about what they just read is a good question. You could even take these questions a step further and ask, "Why?" or "How do you know?" These could be excellent lead-ins to teaching the elements of a story, figurative language, or concepts of print. Basically, you want to get the students talking, in whatever way that works for you. Having conferences with students one-on-one or in small groups during silent reading is also effective. Make sure the questions you ask are not ones that make the students feel as if they are being quizzed.

Teaching Tip

Some questions or leads to try:
1. What made you choose that book?
2. Have you read anything else by this author?
3. How do you like the book so far?
4. Can you tell me about the main character?
5. Do you know where the story takes place?
6. When I read it . . .
7. What I know about that author is . . .
8. I usually choose books by . . .

Be careful when talking to your students that you use vocabulary they understand. I am not implying that you should simplify your words (quite the opposite if you want to encourage them to learn new words), but be aware of your language and make sure it isn't a form of jargon. I had been working as a facilitator at workshops for other teachers all summer. I was using words such as *engagement, modeling, cooperative learning, ability grouping*—words that some call "edubabble." Without realizing it, I had carried some of that language into my classroom. I had planned a book talk for my morning class. One student, who was always disinterested and often had his head down or resting on his hand, was sitting up front. He was a sweet boy who I suspected had a slight crush on me. I started the morning by saying, "Today, I am going to model for you . . ." Before I had a chance to finish by saying "how to give a book talk," this boy yanked his head up, raised his fists in the air in a celebratory manner, and whooped, "You ARE? Awwwwww right!" Apparently, his definition of *modeling* and mine were not the same. Be careful: your students sometimes hang on your every word. If you are lucky, and deliberate with your vocabulary, the conversations begin to take on a productive, wonderful life of their own.

Helping Students Choose Books

Even though I finally accumulated a large classroom library, with a wide variety of genres and reading levels, my students needed help choosing books. I suspect some of your students will need assistance also. Again, don't force your students to read only core literature or books considered "classics." Jim Trelease, in *The Read-Aloud Handbook,* writes, "An interesting thing happened to classics: About the only people in this country who read them are teenagers—and only because they have to" (2001). Let your students choose what they want to read. Help them choose material without requiring certain titles (see Appendix 4).

It isn't enough to read books, put them in your classroom, and recommend them to the class. Students need to be led to the books that are right for them. How do you do that? To reiterate the basics:

■ Gather information about your students' interests through daily conversations, surveys, interviews, or parent surveys. (Pay attention to favorite sports, movies they've seen, hobbies they have, siblings they live with, feelings about parents or family life, TV programs they watch, subjects they like in school, etc.)

■ Learn the range of reading levels in your class. This can be done using state standardized test scores, DRP scores, or any other reliable reading comprehension test. You might ask your guidance counselor or reading specialist for help in obtaining these tests.

- Give book talks on a regular basis and encourage other teachers, administrators, community guests, and students to do the same. Hold "read-ins" and invite guests to read to your students for the first five minutes of class.

- Show your students where books are in the room. Let them take part in organizing and displaying books, magazines, and other reading material. Have a classroom library that is user-friendly. Create a comfortable place where students will want to go to read.

- Let your students help choose the books that will be purchased. This is most easily done by having them circle choices in catalogs or by taking them to the bookstore with you.

- Introduce your students to the school and local library. Go there on a field trip. Pass out information to parents on how to obtain a library card.

- Lead book drives, ask for donations, write grants, and use book clubs to get new books into your classroom on a regular basis.

- Ultimately, let the students choose their own reading selection each day.

Book Passes

In *Yellow Brick Roads,* Janet Allen describes how she found the term "book pass" in Candy Carter and Zora Rashkis's *Ideas for Teaching English in the Junior High and Middle School* (1981). Janet adapted their original idea to meet her own goals. A book pass gives students a quick look at many different books so they can find one they would like to read. You are physically putting books into the hands of students rather than having them go to the shelf with no idea of what is there.

Teaching Tip

Directions for holding a book pass:
- Have students sit in a circle. The number of students in the circle depends on how long you want the pass to last, and how many books you want them exposed to during the pass.

■ Give each student a book pass form.

■ Give a different book to each student. Let each student examine the book for two to three minutes. They should look at the front cover, back cover, and any illustrations, and then actually read the beginning of the book. (Of course, some students will read the ending instead.)

■ Each student then fills out one line on the book pass form (see Appendix 1). The form allows the student to record the title, author, and a rating for each book. My students devised our rating system for each book. Some classes rated the books on a five-star system, and others graded on an A–F scale.

■ Once you see the students have had enough time to peruse the book and complete the book pass form, you say, "Pass."

■ When you say "pass," students pass their books to the right, thereby giving their book to another student and simultaneously receiving a book from the student on their left.

■ The procedure is repeated.

■ The book pass is complete when everyone has his or her original book back.

If you have a circle set up with fewer students than others, place empty chairs in that circle and assign a book to each chair. Instruct the students to act as if a person is there in the seat. This will ensure that your entire class finishes the book pass at the same time, and that there won't be disruptions from students who finish early. You might need to demonstrate how to pass at a circle where there is a missing person. I have held book passes in the past where that got confusing for the students.

The point of the book pass is to actually get books into the hands (and heads) of the students. If you simply guide students to a reading area in your room, they won't always know where to look or what to choose. If you preselect books you think they might like (based on their interests and reading level) and place them in their hands, you have a much better chance of making a match. When I look at my students' reading logs, 90 percent of the time I find books they also have recorded on their book pass sheet. For me, it is a quick, easy way to match books to my students' interests. In Sha-kia's case (see Figure 5.1), it is easy to see that she prefers books with female protagonists. Thomas, on the other hand, appears to like mysteries and

Figure 5.1 Sha-Kia's Book Pass log

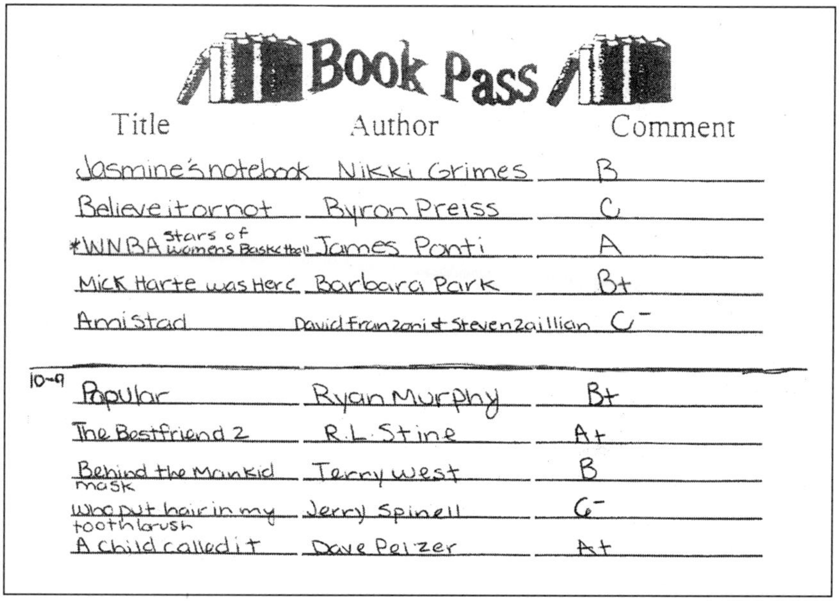
Book Pass

Title	Author	Comment
Jasmine's notebook	Nikki Grimes	B
Believe it or not	Byron Preiss	C
*WNBA Stars of womens Basketball	James Ponti	A
Mick Harte was Here	Barbara Park	B+
Amistad	David Franzoni + Steven Zaillian	C−
10-9 Popular	Ryan Murphy	B+
The Bestfriend 2	R.L. Stine	A+
Behind the Mankid mask	Terry West	B
Who put hair in my toothbrush	Jerry Spinell	C−
A child called it	Dave Pelzer	A+

Figure 5.2 Thomas's Book Pass log

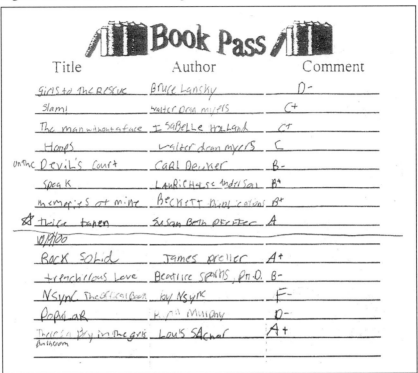

Title	Author	Comment
Girls to The Rescue	Bruce Lansky	D-
Slam!	Walter Dean myers	C+
The man without a face	Isabelle Holland	C+
Hoops	Walter dean myers	C
on the Devil's Court	Carl Deuker	B-
Speak	Laurie Halse Anderson	B+
memories of mine	Beckett Publications	B+
thrice fanen	Susan Beth Pfeffer	A
10/14/00		
Rock Solid	James Preller	A+
treacherous Love	Beatrice Sparks, Ph.D.	B-
Nsync The official Book	by Nsync	F-
Popular	Kim Murphy	D-
There's a boy in the girls Bathroom	Louis Sachar	A+

stories related to sports (see Figure 5.2). This information helps me make better text-student matches for SSL reading time.

Book passes are also an excellent way to determine whether a student is familiar with the parts of a book. I have discovered a multitude of much-needed mini-lesson topics from observing my students participating in a book pass. Once when I asked if anyone had a book they might want to read later, a sixth-grade girl yelled enthusiastically, "I want to read Judy Blume by *Blubber*!" This immediately let me know that she needed help distinguishing between the title and author of a book.

You can also use this method to share professional resources with your department or entire staff. I advocate holding one book pass for new young adult fiction and one for new professional literature each month in your department or grade-level meeting.

Having the Time

I already discussed the parameters for the time you should allow for SSR, so I won't go into that in much detail here. However, I want to stress the point that you need to make time for reading each day. Students should be learning comprehension, decoding, and fluency strategies throughout the day. SSR (or SSL in my case) is where the students will be able to practice what they are learning. It seems that it is easy for schools or individual teachers to deduct from free-reading time, assuming that it is unimportant, or that students will get it in another class or at home. This is especially true when teachers feel there is too much curriculum they need to cover. What goes unrealized is this: students will better understand all content area material once they become better readers. They can become more successful readers through silent reading programs. Often, SSR is the first thing to go when something has to be cut from a schedule. Make sure that doesn't happen in your school or in your classroom.

Reading Aloud

When we read aloud, often and well, we fill our classrooms with
the sound of words, well placed and well written, and that sound
wraps its arms around the work of young writers and readers who
are hard at work learning their craft.
Katie Wood Ray, *Wondrous Words*

Reading aloud is an integral component for any content area class, and your sustained silent reading program should definitely include it. Reading aloud is most often the favorite technique that hooks students and makes them want to read on their own. Jim Trelease, author of *The Read-Aloud Handbook,* actually has a chapter titled "Sustained Silent Reading: Reading-Aloud's Natural Partner."

Reasons to read aloud:

- Build background knowledge
- Provide a model for fluent reading

Teaching Tip

- Expose students to a wide variety of genres
- Make reading pleasurable
- Motivate students to read independently
- Guide students in choosing books
- Develop higher-level thinking skills
- Improve listening skills
- Connect books to students' lives
- Provide examples of new and different writing
- Teach elements of literature
- Lead students in meaningful discussions
- Students learn effective strategies (predicting, questioning, responding, etc.)
- Lead students to a lifelong love of reading!

Choosing Successful Read-Aloud Selections

*Some books are to be tasted, others to be swallowed, and some few
to be chewed and digested: that is, some books are to be read only
in parts, others to be read, but not curiously, and some few to be
read wholly, and with diligence and attention.*
Francis Bacon, *Philosophical Studies*

In choosing your read-aloud selections, again make certain you know the interests of your student and their tolerance level for listening. Haven't you, at one time or another, listened to something being read aloud, only to realize you can't remember a thing about it once it's completed? Your students will get distracted, too. Therefore it is important to select short, interesting pieces to read aloud. Some examples of selections you might want to read include strong leads, descriptive passages, interesting or mysterious settings, humorous anecdotes, bizarre facts, or scary stories. These selections can take the format of a book excerpt, short story, poetry, magazine article, newspaper article, or even e-mail. I once had a story e-mailed to me about two men on a hotel elevator who are regarded suspiciously by another passenger because of their skin color. One of the men says, "Hit the floor," and the third person, thinking she is being robbed, falls hysterically to the floor. The punch line is that one of the men is actually Michael Jordan and he is simply asking that the elevator button be pushed for the floor of his room. I am fairly certain this is a tale, but my students found it highly entertaining. Around election time, people often send e-mails that satirize the candidates. Last year I was sent a song (that I was instructed to sing to the tune of *The Beverly Hillbillies*) about both George W. Bush and Al Gore. This also proved to be a unique, yet immensely popular, read-aloud. See Appendix 4 for some read-aloud selections.

Stating Your Purpose

When reading aloud to your students, make sure they know what the purpose of the read-aloud is, and what you expect from them (their role as student). If you are sharing a story simply for their pleasure, say so. Tell them their only job is to sit back, relax, and enjoy the story. If you want them to listen for certain vocabulary words, or make predictions, or think of questions on a particular topic, tell them before you start reading. It is extremely important that you define the role of the student clearly. Imagine how differently you read a John Grisham novel as opposed to a driver's license manual. Knowing you are responsible for retaining information changes the way you read. It is crucial that we teach students how to change their listening, reading, and writing behaviors to suit their purpose.

Reading Aloud: The Role of the Teacher

Few things are harder to put up with than the annoyance of a good example.
Mark Twain, *Pudd'nhead Wilson*

You will be reading aloud to students who initially might not want to be read to. They may think the idea of hearing a story, whether it pertains to the content area or not, is elementary. Cheryl Sigmon, author of *Modifying the Four Blocks for Upper Grades,* says reading aloud should accomplish the three E's: Entertainment (for the reader and listener), Exposure (to a variety of genres), and Encouragement (to motivate readers) (2001).

Teaching Tip

To make your read-aloud more effective, you need to consider the following:

- Choose something you think students will find interesting.
- Choose something that you also enjoy reading.
- Practice several times before reading it to the class.
- Pause in appropriate places to build suspense.
- Repeat certain phrases or passages, if necessary.
- Do NOT use it as a time to instruct.
- Skip certain parts of the selection if they do not add to the story.
- Watch your timing—do not start reading aloud if you won't have time to finish.
- Read at an appropriate speed and enunciate clearly.
- Provide time for discussions, so students can ask questions.

Pay close attention to the tone and speed you use when you are reading aloud. The first time I read aloud to a class was during a shared reading of *The Lottery Rose*. The students had copies of the book and were following along as I read aloud. I had finished approximately three-quarters of the first chapter when Steven, a boisterous sixth grader, raised his hand and waved it frantically. When I called on him, he said, "Geez, can you please slow down?" Without thinking, I answered, "But Steven, I'm reading it with you— can't you keep up?" To which he replied, "Uhhh . . ., if you didn't notice, we kind of have trouble reading. I believe that's why we're in here." Make sure you don't make the same mistake. Keep in mind that most of your students read at a much slower pace than you. You will need to slow down and possibly reread sections, especially if you are engaged in a true read-aloud, and the students do not have a copy of the text.

Above all, have fun when you read aloud. Your students will be able to tell if you are enjoying what you are reading, and you want to show them that reading is a pleasurable experience.

Reading at Home

Jim Trelease, in *The Read-Aloud Handbook,* writes that he is afraid "We are creating school-time readers, rather than lifetime readers" (2001). I fear that we are not yet creating "school-time" readers. For this reason, I believe it is extremely important to have students read during the school day and continue to read at home. I knew that my students were not doing that, but I also knew it was necessary if I wanted reading to become a part of their lives. I started giving the students home reading logs. You can create these, or you can just use the same reading log the students use in class. (I added a section for a parent signature.) I was a little worried that students would think I was requiring a signature because I didn't believe they were really reading, when actually, I was doing it in an attempt to get parents more involved. I thought it would be a useful vehicle for parents to learn what their students were interested in, what they were choosing to read, and how often they were actually reading. Parents were also easily able to write notes or comments to me on these logs if they had questions or concerns about their students' progress.

I waited until we had an effective SSL program in place before I assigned home reading logs. I have continued using these, but I find they always work better if I wait until the second month of school. By that time, students are in the routine of reading, and they know how to write an appropriate response.

I also had many students who brought in complete home reading logs with beautiful responses but no parent signatures. I accepted these initially, but I always followed up with a phone call to their home. Many students really had no excuse for not having their parents sign, but a few had valid reasons. If you have students who have special circumstances at home that don't allow them to see their parents very often, you may have to make a few exceptions. I had one student who saw his mom only one night a week. The rest of the nights she worked late and he was in bed by the time she came home. I helped them set up the arrangement that the mom would sign several weeks' worth of logs, with the understanding that she trusted that her son was really reading. I also asked her to talk to her son about what he was reading on that one night they spent time together, if she could fit it into her schedule.

Once your students are on their way to becoming readers, you will find they enjoy reading at home. I had one student who even created her own home reading log that she submitted for extra credit (see Figure 5.3). Aside from the scribbled messiness of it, the comments she wrote about the book told me she really was reading it and understanding the story.

Reflections

I was very excited about our new SSL program. I thought the changes were positive contributions to our program, and to our day.

Figure 5.3 Sha-Kia's home reading log

Although I did not analyze my students' test scores that year, I did notice improvements in their DRP scores. Approximately two-thirds of my class increased their DRP score by at least two stanines! The students also voiced how much they appreciated the variety in our schedule, and they were certainly reading and talking about reading more than ever before. Many students checked out books from my classroom library, and several were never returned. Although initially I was slightly angry over the loss of books, I realized what an excellent sign it was that the students actually wanted the books badly enough to keep them.

The writing days were still a bit of a struggle. I decided toward the end of the year to give students prompts on SSW days. This really helped. I wrote three prompts on the board for each SSW day, and I always included "student choice" as one of the prompts to allow for student creativity. The struggling writers really appreciated the support the prompts lent, and they stayed on task more easily than before.

Teaching Tip

Give students writing prompts to give them direction. Always allow one choice to be "student choice."

Possible prompts:

1. When you are striving for something you really want, and you don't get it, do you often quit, or keep trying? What makes you give up? What makes you keep trying?

2. Do you see yourself running for public office one day? Why or why not? If you were elected president, what is the first thing you would do?

3. Are you more likely to hold back your tears when you feel like crying, or hold back laughter when something is funny? Why?

4. Do you wish your parents would question you more or less about what you do and how you feel? Why?

5. If you could change any one thing about the way you look, what would you change? Why?

6. Are you afraid to ask questions when you don't understand something¿ Do you ever fake a laugh when you don't get a joke¿ Why¿

7. Student Choice.

CHAPTER SIX

Promoting Literacy Beyond the Classroom

One's mind once stretched by a new idea never regains its original dimensions.
Oliver Wendell Holmes, Jr., *The Mind and Faith of Justice Holmes*

After three successful years of SSL in my classroom in Florida, I moved to California. I was fortunate enough to be hired by a principal who already believed in giving students time to read. She had a traditional schoolwide SSR program already in place attached to period seven (after lunch) each day, but thought it was completely ineffective.

Because I wasn't sure the elements of a balanced literacy program (reading, writing, and reading aloud) were being used in language arts classes (or any other classes) at this school, I suspected that SSL might work. I also hoped the added variety would alleviate the boredom teachers and students reported from the previous traditional SSR program, as it had in my classroom.

Because teachers and students agreed that ten minutes was not enough time for reading, the SSL period was increased to twenty minutes. The extra minutes were taken (half from each) from our allotted time for homeroom and from the time between classes. To combat postlunch fatigue, SSL was scheduled in the morning, during third period. To prevent it from serving as a way to increase the time in a content area course, SSL became a separate class for which students changed rooms and teachers.

Schoolwide Accountability

For record keeping and assessment, we decided the students should keep folders, which would contain reading logs and writing logs. We used brightly colored folders with three prongs and two inside pockets. These can be purchased in bulk through your school's county office, or from retail stores such as Target, Office Depot, or Price Club. Purchasing these before the start of the school year will save you a lot of money. I have found them as low as eight cents a folder during back-to-school sales.

Students also housed their completed pieces of writing from SSW days in these folders. They were told to write freely without worrying about grammar or spelling mistakes. The writing pieces were graded on presence (according to whether they were actually being written each day). The logs were filled out daily by students and checked weekly by teachers to monitor progress. These folders were kept in the classroom and not taken home, thereby alleviating any possibilities of students forgetting their folders.

Students were assigned a citizenship grade, not an academic one, based on behavior, tardiness, and number of entries in each log. This grade was documented on students' report cards each trimester and used to determine citizenship honors and awards. Team leaders helped create the rubric by determining the number of entries needed each trimester and then converting that number to a percentage, which would be applied to our existing schoolwide grading scale (see Appendix 3). Students, teachers, and parents were given these rubrics before the course began so they would know what was expected of them.

The Schedule

All teachers of all content areas were assigned an SSL class. Teachers in the language arts department and I modeled how to set them up. I was originally not assigned an SSL class so I could be available to others who might want or need my support. SSL still took place during third period and followed this schedule:

- Mondays, Tuesdays, and Wednesdays: SSR (Sustained Silent Reading)

- Thursday: SSW (Sustained Silent Writing)

- Friday: RA (Read-Aloud)

Professional Development

Teachers were asked to participate in training approximately once per trimester where they were given ideas and the ability to share comments and strategies on classroom management, motivation, and assessment. These training sessions occurred on campus and were very informal. I also shared (or asked others to share) a successful strategy or tip at our staff meeting each week. This became routine and was listed as the "SSL Minute" on our staff meeting agendas.

Teachers were also given weekly packets filled with daily schedules that contained suggested writing prompts for the SSW days as well as an optional read-aloud selection (poem, article, short story, novel excerpt, etc.) for RA days. This later changed to a monthly schedule to help cut down on copying costs.

Teaching Tip

Provide your staff with sample monthly SSL schedules:

Thursday: SSW
Choose One:
1. Do you remember being read to as a child? What did your parents read to you? What is your favorite story?

2. What is the best thing you did over the holiday break? Why was it the best?

3. Student choice

Friday: RA
Read the attached short story, "Moon Over Missouri," from Donald Gallo's *No Easy Answers,* or have a student read aloud. Preview and practice first!

Thursday: SSW
Choose One:
1. Would you rather be a rich and famous movie star or a doctor who saves a lot of people, but who is not wealthy or well known? Why?

2. Of all the nice things someone could truthfully say about you, which one would make you feel the best? Why?

3. Student choice

Friday: RA
Read (or have a student read) the attached story, "The All-American Slurp," from Donald Gallo's *Visions*. Practice first!

Thursday: SSW
1. Tomorrow is the spelling bee. Do you wish you were in it? Why or why not?

> 2.   What do you choose in a game of truth and dare—truth or dare? Why? Do you ever pick the other? When and why?
>
> 3.   Student choice
>
> **Friday: RA**
> Read the excerpt from Jerry Spinelli's *Wringer,* or have a student read. Practice first!

The read-aloud selection could be read by the teacher, a student (only if they practiced first), or a guest reader (another teacher, a parent, an administrator, district personnel, or a community member). See Appendix 3 for more information and sample SSL schedules.

The weekly packet for the first week of school contained information and suggestions on how to set up the folders, where to store them, and the logistics on passing them out and collecting them.

Observations/Problems

Because I was responsible for a lot of the decisions about changing the existing reading program (with the consensus of only a small committee), the staff initially seemed resistant. It was difficult as a young, new teacher to reach a staff that was filled with so many experienced teachers. I think that having me involved and acting somewhat "in charge" of SSL might have had some detrimental effects. Change was hard enough for the staff without having someone completely new to the school and district introduce it.

Some teachers thought the idea of having SSL as a separate class was a waste of time—that having a passing period for a twenty-minute class was ridiculous. Others liked the class being separate and thought the students were taking it more seriously because of it.

The other problem was student and teacher accountability. Teachers wanted the students held accountable, thus the need for folders and citizenship grades. Some teachers, however, did not like the idea of having to take extra time to read and grade the folders. It was also said that because the writing pieces were not being graded for grammar errors, the students would not really be gaining anything in relation to writing. There was also no way of knowing whether teachers were really reading and checking the folders, or if they were giving grades based on classroom observation or personal opinion. The principal thought that not all of the teachers were modeling reading and writing during SSL, but were instead using the time to grade papers or take care of other matters. She also worried that teachers needed more training and perhaps help, but weren't asking for it. She asked me to use SSL as a time to visit other classrooms. However, what was intended to be a way of helping teachers was perceived by some as a monitoring device. Teachers began to feel that they were being "policed," and understandably, they started to resent it. Therefore I began to go into classrooms only when I was invited, or I tried to invite myself into classes where I knew the teacher would not mind my being there. I did not want anyone to feel threatened by my presence because I knew that would not benefit teachers or students, or help the reading program in any way.

In addition, the materials we purchased were not entirely appropriate. Because we initially bought books in "grab bag" fashion, we were not able to choose specific titles. A book club magazine offered a "grab bag" of a hundred books for ninety-nine dollars. These were great titles, just not great matches with our population of students. We purchased these somewhat hastily in our zeal to get books into rooms. Therefore, not all our books were suited to match the needs, interests, language, or reading levels of our students. We knew that, if we wanted to continue the program, we would need to purchase more books, as well as magazines, picture books, and newspaper subscriptions.

Books/Materials

To get more materials, we decided to hold a book drive. Our school comprises seven teams: three for seventh grade, three for eighth grade, and one mixed seventh- and eighth-grade team. Teams consist of six teachers (one from each content area, including electives) and approximately 150 students. These teams competed against each other in a friendly contest to collect the most books. The book drive lasted the first three weeks of school. Approximately 1,500 books were collected. We sorted the books and took any inappropriate ones to used bookstores to trade. Those that could not be traded were donated to Goodwill.

The principal then allotted each team $900 to spend on books, magazines, picture books, and newspapers. The entire $900 could be spent at the beginning of the year, or teams could save some and spread it throughout the year. Most used the money right away. I offered many recommendations and provided young adult book lists, but ultimately, each teacher made the decision on what was purchased for his or her classroom. Teachers also had the opportunity to ask students what they wanted to be ordered. This eliminated the lack of variety in books that we had had the previous year. Teachers on the same team were encouraged to order different books so they could rotate them among team members. Display racks were also purchased for each room so that magazines and/or picture books could be arranged in a way that would be appealing and accessible to students. Some teachers used part of the money to buy more furniture such as beanbags and big pillows to create comfortable reading areas.

Test Scores

I analyzed our test scores by grade level. Consistent with my belief that students need prolonged amounts of time to read, and that this time must be provided regularly, the best results (the largest increase in reading scores) occurred after a group of students had experienced at least two consecutive years of SSL. This can be determined when examining the scores of the class of 2000, which was filled with students who had been at our school for both years of SSL. They had more increases (23 percent to 34 percent) in reading scores than the class of 1999 (25 percent to 28 percent), who had been at our school for only one year of SSL (see Figure 6.1).

Both classes of students also showed increases in language scores. These increases were present in the National Percentile Ranking (NPR) as well as the percentage of students who scored at or above the fiftieth percentile. The average reading comprehension

Figure 6.1 Record and analyze important information to measure improvement in your students

	National Percentile Ranking (NPR)			
	Class of 1999		Class of 2000	
	Grade 7	Grade 8	Grade 7	Grade 8
	(1997–98)	(1998–99)	(1998–99)	(1999–2000)
Reading	25	28	23	34
Language	30	35	34	37

	Stanford Achievement Test Results Percent at or Above the 50th Percentile			
	Class of 1999		Class of 2000	
	Grade 7	Grade 8	Grade 7	Grade 8
	(1997–98)	(1998–99)	(1998–99)	(1999–2000)
Reading	22	23	20	32
Language	30	32	32	34

score and language score from the most recent class (the class of 2001) again rose approximately 40 percent (see Figure 6.2). These are not exact matched sets and scores do not reflect student mobility.

Student and Teacher Feedback

Consistent with my classroom practice, I distributed surveys to teachers and students to get feedback about SSL (see Appendix 2). The students overwhelmingly loved read-aloud days the best. Teachers were split, half liking the reading days, and half enjoying the read-aloud days. Teachers and students ranked the writing day as the one they liked the least. Although some teachers shared successful experiences, most thought SSW was the hardest day to motivate the students and to control behavior.

In regard to time, ten teachers thought that twenty minutes was enough time for SSL, whereas seven thought it was not enough time, and one wrote that it was too much time. Thirteen teachers wrote that they used the packets given to them each week, two teachers responded that they did not use the packets, and three left that ques-

Figure 6.2

National Percentile Ranking (NPR)		
	Class of 2001	
	Grade 7	Grade 8
	(2000–01)	
Reading Comprehension	26	37
Language	34	41

tion blank. There were mixed responses about using the SSL folders. Seven teachers liked having the folders, seven did not like them, and three left that question blank.

When asked what their students read the most, six wrote "books," four said "magazines," and eight said "a variety." When asked whether the students were volunteering to read aloud, there were six "yes" responses, six "no" responses, and six responses of "sometimes."

Teachers reported that they were modeling appropriate behavior during SSL class. Sixteen teachers said they always modeled reading and writing, and only two answered that they did "sometimes."

As far as whether teachers wanted SSL to continue next year, fourteen wrote "yes," two wrote "no," and two wrote "¿" The only suggestions written on how to change SSL were to eliminate grading it, and to remove the SSW day.

All in all, I was pleased with the responses from the teachers. The only thing that discouraged me was the number of surveys that were not returned. I really wanted teacher feedback, and tried to be nonthreatening about it. Teachers did not have to put their names on the surveys, and I gave them approximately three weeks to fill them out. (I even suggested they fill them out on a Thursday, during SSW.) In the future, I will distribute them earlier in the year. As we all know, the end of the school year is not always the most convenient time to get things done.

Reflections

The schoolwide SSL program was successful, and I felt good about its implementation. Students and teachers were positive about the program, test scores in reading comprehension increased, and more books were being read than in previous years. I could see growth in the students in my class. One girl happened to be in the same SSL class for two consecutive years, first as a seventh grader, and then as an eighth grader. I can actually look at her reading and writing logs and determine how much she has changed as a reader (see Figures 6.3 and 6.4). The reading choices she is making, the topics she chooses to write on, and the amount of writing she is doing is apparent. These logs should also be useful for the teachers she has in future years.

In one SSL class, as a writing topic, I gave students the choice of writing what they thought of our SSL program. Tania wrote a reflection I found to be very honest and encouraging (see Figure 6.5).

Figure 6.3 Diana's reading log, grade 7

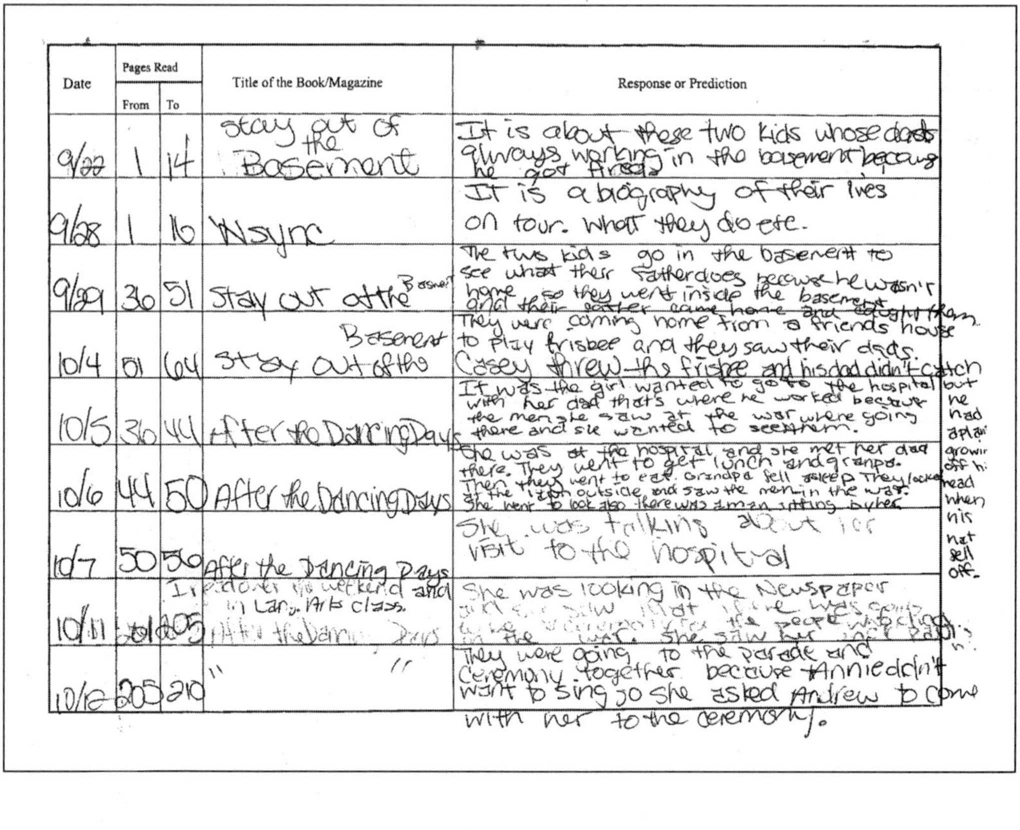

Figure 6.4 Diana's reading log, grade 8

Date	Pages Read From	Pages Read To	Title of the Book/Magazine	Response or Prediction
9/7			The Lost Boy	Browsing through it.
9/11	1	5	The Lost Boy	He was still being tortured by his mom. .
9/13	1	13	Falling Up	Various Poems
9/15	13	19	Falling Up	Various Poems
9/18	1	14	Chicken Soup for the Teenage Soul III	Dear Boy / Dear Girl
9/19			P.E. Handbook & Study for P.E. Test	Study for Test
9/20			I Love you, I Hate you, not lost	Ms. Marshall Read
9/25	14	18	Chicken Soup for the teenage Soul III	I Had to let him Go
9/30			SCL Book orders	SCL Book Orders

Figure 6.5 Tania's reflections

SSL Reflections
In my SSL class I really enjoy these things:
I like read aloud day better because it's the
day when you don't read and you relax
and listen to the teacher read. My reading
has improved because of SSR it has
improved because I read much faster. My
writing has improved with ssw because
I like writting and I write intresting
thing. I have enjoyed SSL because it's
quiet and it's a time with peace. The
changes that I will suggest for next
year is to 2 reading days, 2 writting
days and 1 read aloud day.

Connections

Teachers often ask if it is okay for students to do book reports in SSL. I have never required these of my students (nor will I ever) because I did not want them to feel as though they were being "tested" on the book they were reading. I simply wanted them to enjoy reading. Several of my students started showing their understanding of books in other ways. The connections they were making between the text and their own interests surprised me. For instance, several phenomenal artists in one class began creating beautiful maps, time lines, and caricatures based on the stories they were reading (see Figure 6.6). I saw that they were really making meaning out of the text—reading was finally making sense to them!

The Need for Ongoing Professional Development

I do not think we provided enough staff development for the teachers on how to continue to operate SSL. Our state recently passed laws about retaining students, and our school was in the position of having to retain students for the first time. With that came a lot of responsibility and paperwork, which, understandably, became our central focus for much of the year.

As I look at continuing SSL in upcoming years, I am meeting with my principal to try to find open dates on our calendar for ongoing professional development. This is important so we can discuss and attempt to solve new problems, but also so our new teachers (of which we have many each year) can learn how to effectively operate SSL in their classrooms.

I believe that anything worth doing takes time, and deserves the opportunity for reflection, analysis, change, and support. For many teachers and students, SSL was a completely new and somewhat foreign experience. The reading, writing, and speaking that I was asking everyone to participate in did not necessarily come naturally to them. Students needed time to get used to the program, and to voice their thoughts and opinions about it. Teachers needed the same and much more. For non–language arts content area teachers, being

Figure 6.6 Josh's map of setting from reading *Max the Mighty* by Rodman Philbrick

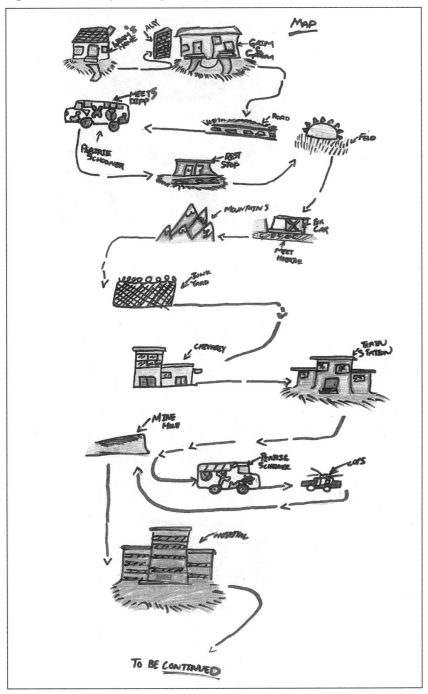

asked to talk about and actually read young adult books was a huge challenge. The staff needed support, and the reinforcement needed to be constant and ongoing.

If I had it to do over, I would enlist a larger team of teachers to act as a support staff for SSL. This is one of my goals for the future. If you are interested in expanding your sustained silent reading time to a schoolwide program, I strongly suggest you recruit your language arts department, or any other interested and capable individuals to help lead the cause. The more people you have to promote reading, suggest titles, raise funds, purchase books, copy logs, talk to students, read aloud, and handle anything else that comes up, the better your program will be.

Promoting Literacy Beyond SSL

You must be the change you wish to see in the world.
Mahatma Gandhi, *The Essential Gandhi* (Fischer)

In addition to implementing a schoolwide SSL program, we did a lot of other things to promote literacy that may or may not have had an effect on our positive results. In response to the student surveys at the beginning of the year, and recommendations from the staff, the following strategies, ideas, and events were implemented:

■ Parents, students, staff, and community members were invited to Family Literacy Night, where teachers shared strategies on how to motivate students to read, how to quickly estimate the reading level of a text, and information on how to obtain library cards. We also raffled almost fifty different reading selections (books, magazines, and dictionaries) so parents and students would have materials to read at home.

■ At staff and department meetings throughout the year, the staff celebrated literacy through talking about literacy strategies, creating and sharing book lists, giving book talks, asking challenging questions, and sharing motivational tactics. These sharing sessions were completely voluntary, but turned out to be very rewarding. One of the best department meetings of the year was when everyone brought a write-up of a successful strategy they use in their classroom. We swapped copies and shared how to teach the strategy to students.

■ A "read-in" was planned to celebrate the birthday of Dr. Seuss. Parents, teachers, community members, and students volunteered to travel to other classrooms and act as guest readers. They chose, practiced, and read aloud their favorite reading selection to the class they were visiting. Books were also given to the readers as gifts of appreciation.

■ A professional library was started for teachers so they could check out books and read the latest research and strategies. I typed up a list of the books with descriptions, housed them in my room, and made them available to be checked out. Unfortunately, only four teachers checked out books (and only seven different titles were used). It is unclear why we had so few teachers take advantage of this library, and I am considering moving it out of my room to a more accessible place. I would like to explore further what we can do to get teachers more interested in reading professional books.

■ A book club was organized for staff members who were interested in reading young adult literature. I knew that if we could get the teachers reading great books, they would feel more comfortable recommending those titles to the students. Out of fifty-five staff members, twenty-four joined the book club. We started late in the year, and read only four books, but we already have a schedule set up for next year.

■ We also created a great young adult literature summer reading list for the teachers and the students. This had not been done in quite a while. The teachers gave students these lists at the end of the year, encouraging them to read over the summer. We did not make it mandatory that students read any books or complete any assignments over the summer; reading from the list was completely optional. We are considering changing that policy and requiring our incoming seventh graders to read one book from the list, and incoming eighth graders to read two books from the list before the start of the school year. The language arts staff have also discussed assigning a written response, but exact criteria for that has not yet been decided.

Additional Support

Fortunately, my principal shared my vision of "meeting students where they are" and working together to hook them as lifelong readers. She was the determining factor in my accepting the position of reading specialist, and the reason I was able to implement so many different strategies in our classrooms and throughout the school. The unconditional support she gave me throughout those years kept me sane and productive.

I have learned that it is vital to have others at your workplace who have philosophies that match your own, especially when trying to start a new program, and even more so if you need the cooperation or funding from others to execute it. My district and school have been, and continue to be, very accommodating in providing support (emotionally and monetarily) for programs that are committed to improving literacy.

Above all else, I am struck by the passion I still feel for improving literacy and making this SSL even more successful. I don't want to abandon the programs we've started, as so many programs in education have been abandoned in the past. When I see students bursting with pride over finishing their first novel, or beaming with joy at being given a new book, I am reminded of just how important my role is as a teacher of reading. It's no wonder teachers and students come to love SSL. Katie Wood Ray says it best in her book *Wondrous Words* (1999):

> I remember the first time I realized students were gazing up at me while I was reading to them. I was overcome for a moment at how significant their gaze was, at how much trust I saw in their upturned faces. At how awesome my responsibility was to fill that space between them and me with words, wondrous words that would not disappoint them, words that would not let them down, words that they and I could stand on, walk across and meet one another in a place the ordinary words of our days forbid us to go. It was a journey of words we could make together through reading. (p. 67)

CHAPTER SEVEN

Frequently Asked Questions on Maintaining SSL

Think long and move slowly but always move forward. By this I mean, think about what you want to see happening in your school three to five years from now and begin working to get there. Change is hard. Change is anxiety-provoking and necessarily slow. My own experience suggests that when we try to change everything at once, little that matters actually changes. But someone has to initiate and support the needed change. If not you, who? If not today, when?
Richard Allington, *What Really Matters for Struggling Readers*

Frequently Asked Questions

Many teachers have asked me about creating and maintaining an SSL program in their own classroom. Below are some of their most frequently asked questions.

What made you create SSL?

Traditional SSR programs didn't work for my students. My students weren't really reading. I knew something was missing; it just took many conversations and periods of observations to uncover what my students truly needed. They needed more than just uninterrupted time to read. The variation of elements (reading, writing, and reading aloud) provided the necessary extra stimulation. They needed to hear a fluent reader read exciting material aloud to them so they would become interested in choosing books on their own. They also needed a stress-free, grade-free avenue such as SSW to clarify their thoughts and consider themselves literate, contributing members of the classroom.

Is your program really that different from traditional SSL programs?

Yes! My students can all tell you it is vastly different. Having three days of reading instead of five is a huge difference to a struggling middle school reader. Having a day where you can relax and simply listen to an entertaining story is fun for students in my classes. Knowing that they took part in the planning and that their voices and opinions matter is also a huge benefit. My students hated SSR and they love SSL. That in itself is the biggest, most important difference of all.

Did the varied curriculum—the added elements of reading aloud and writing—prove effective?

I think the added elements were very beneficial in holding the students' interest level and preventing them from becoming bored. From the survey responses of the teachers and the students, the varied curriculum within SSL was working. The read-aloud days encouraged the students to read. It exposed them to a variety of texts, and created an enthusiasm for reading that had not been there before. I believe that a silent reading program does not always have to be silent. Adding voices to our program by allowing students to talk about books, encouraging students to talk to each other about what they read, and having someone modeling fluent reading each week is invaluable.

The research supports giving students time to write—time with little or no pressure of being graded. However, the success of our writing day and the pleasure, or lack thereof, that the students and teachers derived from it are questionable. In planning for next year's SSL class, that is something we need to take into consideration.

Does SSL work only for struggling readers?

No! After implementing my program schoolwide, we discovered that students in higher-level classes also showed improvement, and, more important, reported increased enjoyment in SSL as well. In fact, these students do not usually need as much motivation to read, and often help motivate and influence their classmates.

How can I provide the best reading program for my students?

My SSL program has been in existence for three years, and each year it had to be tweaked slightly to best fit the needs of our students. I think it has also gotten better with each passing year. You need to find out where your students are in their quest for literacy and meet them at that point. Dealing with students who are preadolescent, or in their teenage years, means they are constantly changing. Therefore you need constant reflection, evaluation, and openness to change. Get to know your students and find out what they need and what they like or are interested in. Use surveys, talk to them, talk to their parents, study their cumulative folder, and talk to their former teachers. Then use that information to build your program around them.

How long should a silent reading program continue?

In the past seven years, I have noticed an upsetting trend. In education, it seems that states, districts, and schools tend to respond quickly and enthusiastically to strategies, ideas, and programs when they are new. But they are abandoned after only a short amount of time if results are not immediately extraordinary. It is only logical that any significant change will require significant time. I want to see SSL continue indefinitely for many reasons. We were able to see improvements in a short amount of time. Imagine what we might see if the students continued to improve at that rate.

Can SSL be used in elementary and high schools?

SSL can be used in any school at any level. Pay attention to the population you are serving and meet the students where they are in regard to reading and writing. Make sure you prepare the classroom and the students for SSL before you start it. You might also secure support and funding before initiating the program in your classroom or throughout your school. If you are unsure whether your particular population of students will respond to SSL, why not try it in a pilot classroom first?

Will a schoolwide SSL program really work?

My answer is an emphatic yes! Initially, in the first year of SSL, there might be resistance to change on the part of both teachers and students. In subsequent years, the amount of productive talk (teacher to student, teacher to teacher, and student to student) that transpires about books and reading will be noticeable. Teachers' and students' attitudes should become much more positive than they have been in the past, and the students' reading scores, especially for those who participate in SSL for consecutive years, should definitely increase. As a whole, my SSL program was successful in promoting literacy, and it gives me hope that positive changes can continue to occur everywhere.

What are the most important elements of SSL?

I believe that a varied curriculum, a knowledgeable teacher, and access to books are the most critical elements of SSL. Students at all reading levels need to be reading for prolonged periods of time, and we cannot always ensure that that is happening away from school. To hook students into becoming lifelong readers, I suggest participating in an SSL class that contains writing and reading aloud. Knowing your students and becoming an avid reader yourself is also crucial. Finally, you must build a classroom library so all students have access to captivating literature.

How do I know which books to read?

The mantra I follow is, Read everything! Seriously, use the Web sites I've documented in Appendix 5, ask colleagues, attend professional workshops, read professional books, and frequent the library and bookstore. No matter what you choose to read, you can't go wrong. There will always be someone out there for whom that book is a perfect match. Start by reading what sounds good to you. You'll be surprised to see that students sometimes like the same topics!

What's the hardest part about running SSL?

SSL isn't hard to create in your classroom, if you are organized and establish a routine from the beginning. The hardest part for me was finding the funding to continue purchasing books for my students. I suggest you borrow, rotate, frequent garage sales, and write grants. Needing more books was actually good and bad. I wanted students to read, but the more they read, the more books I needed to buy. Eventually, your students will get so excited about reading, they will want to purchase books on their own. For students who are not financially able to do that, you will notice they suddenly are interested in finding the public library.

How do you get the teachers and students excited about SSL?

This will depend on your school environment. Having the support of administration is critical. You also need to be enthusiastic yourself. Try reading interesting excerpts aloud at staff meetings, or volunteer to be a guest reader in someone else's class. Once students hear wonderful selections they will get excited about reading. Once teachers see how enthusiastic the students are, they will more than likely join your cause. It is also important to back up your ideas with research. Provide pertinent research information to any teacher doubting the program.

What basic guidelines should I have for my own SSL program?

I recommend the following essential criteria in starting your own program:

- Know why you are starting a silent reading program.

- Ensure that you have the support of administration and staff.

- Plan the schedule so students have at least twenty minutes of time to read.

■ Talk to students (and possibly staff) about what they want. Allow students to choose what to read.

■ Determine the reading level of your students and purchase appropriate materials.

■ For classroom libraries, obtain a large number of books on a variety of topics at many different reading levels.

■ Encourage students to talk about what they are reading—SSR does not always have to be completely silent.

■ Set aside money for ordering books before the year starts and for midyear purchases. Also allot money for ordering paper, photocopying, purchasing folders, and other materials.

■ Decide on your expectations for the students and explain them before the program begins.

■ Plan for at least one read-aloud day per week.

■ For schoolwide programs, provide teachers with read-aloud selections, at least initially. Choose stories, poems, or excerpts that are interesting and captivating. Practice reading first.

I am not suggesting that my SSL program alone is the panacea for poor literacy skills in students. I do believe, though, that it is a start, and that SSL is valid and useful. Children need to see, hear, and experience the value of reading. They need to be given time to read, a variety of materials to choose from, a schedule that is intellectually stimulating rather than boring, the opportunity to respond to what they read, and the exposure to fluent reading. We, as teachers, cannot ensure that this is happening at home, or even in classes (or schools) where we do not personally teach. We must therefore strive to make it happen in our own schools, with our own students, whenever and wherever we can. I am convinced that we must believe and act as Emily Dickinson when she wrote, "Not knowing when the dawn will come, open every door" (Johnson 1976).

Appendixes

Appendix 1: Forms
Daily Reading Log
Writing Log
Book Pass Form

Appendix 2: Surveys
Student Survey
Parent Survey
End-of-the-Year Student SSL Survey
End-of-the-Years Teacher SSL Survey

Appendix 3: Tools to Implement SSL
What Is SSL?
What Is SSR?
What Is SSW?
What Is RA?
SSL Guidelines
SSL Grading Scale
Logistics of SSL
Sample SSL Schedules: A Year at a Glance

Appendix 4: Titles for Teens
Favorite Young Adult Literature Titles
Content Area Titles
Favorite Read-Aloud Selections
Popular Audiobooks
Favorite Short Story Collections

Forms

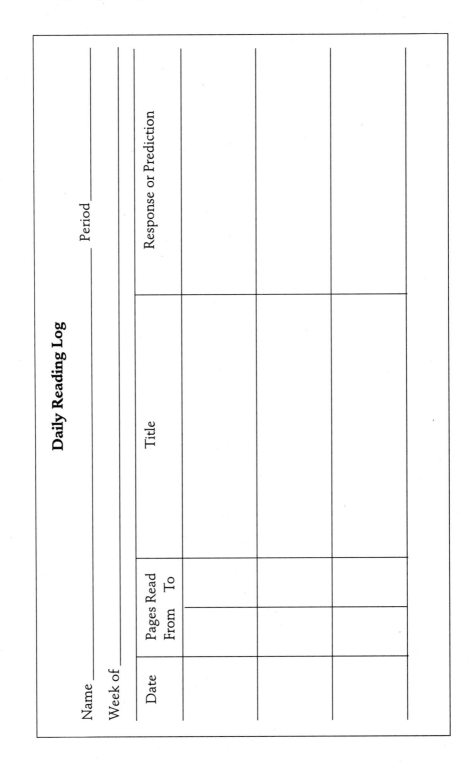

Daily Reading Log

Name _____   Period _____

Week of _____

Date	Pages Read From	To	Title	Response or Prediction

Writing Log

Name _____

Date	Prompt (title of writing)

Book Pass

Name _____

Title	Author	Rating (A–F)

Surveys

Student Survey

Name _____

1. Has anyone ever talked with you individually about the following:
    a: your writing   no   yes
    b: a book you've read   no   yes
    c: your journal   no   yes
    d: your goals/future plans   no   yes
    e: your classes   no   yes
    f: you as a person   no   yes
2. What are your favorite classes in school?
3. What are your least favoriate classes?
4. What do you think are the most important qualities for a teacher to have?
5. What books have you read in the past few years?
6. What is your favorite book?
    What makes this book special?
    Do you have a favorite author? If so, what makes this person a good author?
7. What have you disliked about previous reading/English classes?
    What could have made the class better?
8. What have you enjoyed about previous English classes?
9. How important do you consider reading to be in your life?
    not very   important   extremely
    important   important
10. How important do you consider writing to be in your life?
    not very   important   extremely
    important   important
11. How would you rate yourself as a reader?
    below average   average   above average
12. How would you rate yourself as a writer?
    below average   average   above average
13. Do you consider yourself (a) a better reader than writer (b) a better writer
    than reader (c) equally good in both reading and writing?
14. Who do you know that is a good reader?
15. What do you think has made this person a good reader?
16. What does this person do that makes you think he/she is a good reader?
17. Which of these remarks comes closest to the way you feel about reading?
    a: "I hate reading."

b: "Reading is something you do if someone makes you, but I don't enjoy it."

c: "Reading is OK. Sometimes I pick things up to read."

d: "I like to read but have a hard time with it."

e: "I really enjoy reading and often read when I have free time."

18. Please check all that you like to read.

_____ plays   _____ newspapers

_____ young adult novels   _____ magazines

_____ bestsellers   _____ westerns

_____ nonfiction   _____ romances

_____ fiction   _____ historical fiction

_____ poetry   _____ biographies

19. Which of the following have you written in the past six months?

a: a letter to a friend   f: a poem

b: a business letter   g: a short story

c: a request for something   h: an essay

d: a personal journal or diary   i: lyrics for a song

e: an academic journal

20. What do you think I could do to help you become a better reader?

21. What could you do to become a better reader?

22. What could I do to help you become a better writer?

23. What could you do to become a better writer?

24. What is your favorite movie and what did you particularly like about this movie?

25. What magazines do you like to read?

26. What are your favorite television shows?

Classroom Activities—Please check those that you enjoy.

_____ reading silently   _____ working in a small group

_____ reading   _____ working alone

_____ having someone read to you   _____ completing worksheets, workbooks

_____ writing in journals   _____ doing vocabulary, dictionary work

_____ watching movies   _____ class discussions

_____ listening to cassettes (stories,   _____ writing

      poetry)   _____ publishing your writing (classroom

_____ working as a whole class   magazine, etc.)

Parent Survey

1. What is your child interested in?
   - ___ sports
   - ___ music
   - ___ fashion
   - ___ school
   - ___ friends
   - ___ shopping
   - ___ movies
   - ___ other

2. How often does your child read at home?
   ___ often   ___ sometimes   ___ rarely   ___ never

3. Is your child a good reader?
   ___ yes   ___ no
   Why do you think so?

4. What does your child like to read?
   - ___ romance novels
   - ___ newspapers
   - ___ poetry
   - ___ comics
   - ___ horror stories
   - ___ magazines
   - ___ mysteries
   - ___ short stories
   - ___ sports stories
   - ___ humorous stories
   - ___ other

5. Do you read at home?
   ___ yes   ___ no

6. How often does your child see you reading?
   ___ often   ___ sometimes   ___ rarely   ___ never

7. Did you read aloud to your child when he/she was younger?
   ___ often   ___ sometimes   ___ rarely   ___ never

8. What would you like to see your child do as a reader that he or she does not do now?

9. What are three things your child does well?

10. What are three things your child struggles with?

End-of-the-Year Student SSL Survey

1. What do you like best about SSL: the SSR (reading) days, the SSW (writing) days, or the RA (read-aloud) day? Please explain why.

2. Do you think the current amount of time allotted for SSL (15–20 minutes) is enough, too much, or too little? Please explain.

3. Do you think you understand what you read more now than at the beginning of the year? How do you know?

4. Have you gotten better grades this year in language arts than you did last year?

5. Are you reading more? At home or at school?

6. Do you enjoy reading more than you did before SSL?

7. Do you enjoy writing more than you did before SSL?

8. Do you like SSL? Why or why not?

9. Would you like to have SSL next year? Why or why not?

10. What changes would you make to SSL for next year?

End-of-the-Year Teacher SSL Survey

1. What do you like best about SSL: the SSR (reading) days, the SSW (writing) day, or the RA (read-aloud) day? Please explain why.

2. Do you think the current amount of time allotted for SSL (20 minutes) is enough, too much, or too little? Please explain.

3. Did you use the packets given to you each week?

4. Did you like having the folders for SSL?

5. Did you use the reading selections provided for you?

6. What did your students read the most?

7. Did your students volunteer to read aloud on Fridays?

8. Did you participate by modeling reading and writing for the students?

9. Would you like to have SSL next year? Why or why not?

10. What changes would you make to SSL for next year?

Tools to Implement SSL

What Is SSL?

- SSL is a twenty-minute class period (third period each day) designed to get students excited about reading, writing, and speaking effectively.
- Every teacher on campus is assigned an SSL class made up of students on their team.
- It should be fun (NOT stressful) for the student AND the teacher.
- SSL represents a balanced literacy program and has three components: SSR, SSW, and RA.

What Is SSR?

- Sustained Silent Reading: Students are able to read books, magazines, newspapers, etc., of their choice. They record pages they read on a reading log. *SSR takes place each Monday, Tuesday, and Wednesday.*
- Teachers should read during SSR, and make book recommendations to students. Let students make recommendations as well.
- Teachers should give book talks and encourage students to have discussions (share) about what they are reading.

What Is SSW?

- Sustained Silent Writing: Students write on given prompts and place their work in a folder. A writing log is also filled out to keep track of writing entries. Students are encouraged to free-write, and are NOT graded on grammar, mechanics, etc. *SSW takes place each Thursday.*
- Teachers should have prompts on the board or overhead in the same place each week for students to use in their writing.

- Teachers should also write during SSW.
- Teachers and students should talk about the writing. Sharing written pieces is also encouraged.

What Is RA?

Read-Aloud Day: Students listen to a selection being read aloud, simply for pleasure. Students may also volunteer to read aloud for others. Any reader must practice first.

SSL Guidelines

Supporting Student Literacy (SSL) is held during third period campuswide. The goal is to create a time period where the entire school consists of classrooms filled with students who are reading, writing, and speaking (about books). It is a twenty-minute course, taught by a team teacher, designed to create a love for literacy. To be literate is to read, write, and communicate effectively. Therefore this course has three important components:

- (SSR) Sustained Silent Reading (Monday, Tuesday, and Wednesday)
- (SSW) Sustained Silent Writing (Thursday)
- (RA) Read-Alouds (Friday)

Students are to keep folders (which are given to them) that contain reading logs and writing logs. These stay in the classrooms so they won't be lost or forgotten. Students are required to record the pages they have read on reading days, and keep logs of their writing pieces on writing days. On Fridays, (Read-Aloud day) they may volunteer to participate in a read-aloud, or they may listen to the person reading to them. All students must participate in SSL, as it is a separate course and will appear as such on their report card. Although no homework is assigned in SSL classes, we strongly encourage family support of reading at home. The following guidelines are requirements for students during their SSL class:

Participation: Students are expected to come to class on time ready to read, write, and communicate effectively. The class is only twenty minutes long, so there is no time to waste.

Materials: Students will need paper to write on, and a pen or pencil. Folders and logs will be provided for them.

Behavior: All school rules (code of conduct), team rules, and classroom rules must be followed.

Books: Each student will need a book or magazine to read on SSR days. Books may be selected from the classroom library or school library. However, students are also encouraged to bring their own (appropriate) reading material, and/or use the school or local library. Donations of books, magazines, and newspapers are also always welcome.

Grading: Use the grading guidelines to determine a passing grade.

SSL Grading Scale

Each trimester during their SSL class, students have the opportunity to read (and fill out reading logs) on 36 days, write (and fill out writing logs) on approximately 12 days, and listen to 12 read-alouds. Because we are trying to develop a love for writing, we do not grade the writing pieces for grammar, spelling, or other syntax errors.

O (Outstanding)

■ Students demonstrate outstanding participation in SSL class. The (combined) reading/writing logs must have 42–48 complete, legible entries. They must also have no more than two unexcused tardies. Students listen attentively during Read-Aloud days.

S (Satisfactory)

■ Students demonstrate satisfactory participation in SSL class. The (combined) reading/writing logs must have 35–41 complete, legible entries. In addition, they may have only three to four unexcused tardies. Students listen often during Read-Aloud days.

N (Needs Improvement)

■ Students demonstrate below-average participation in SSL class. The (combined) reading/writing logs have only 28–34 complete, legible entries. In addition, they may have only five to six unexcused tardies. Students usually listen during Read-Aloud days.

U (Unsatisfactory)

■ Students demonstrate unsatisfactory participation in SSL class. The (combined) reading/writing logs contain 27 or fewer complete, legible entries. In addition, they have been tardy seven or more times.

With genuine effort on the part of the student, in addition to parental support at home, this can be a fun-filled, valuable learning experience for us all. Encourage SSL. Encourage literacy. Encourage reading!

Logistics of SSL

Information and Tips

- Each teacher should have a class library in his or her room. If you have changed rooms, or are new to the school, ask your team to share their books, or try to find the previous teacher so you can find the SSL books. I do not yet know if we will have money to order more books this year.
- All magazines that came in over the summer have been delivered to the library. Those will be divided and given to team leaders to be distributed among the team. I do not yet know if we have money to order magazines, or renew previous subscriptions.
- Folders, reading logs, and writing logs will be delivered to your room as soon as they arrive. A master copy of the reading and writing logs is in the front office (in a mailbox on the top row) for you to use to recopy throughout the year.
- Students get only one folder for the entire year. If a student leaves your SSL class, please allow him or her to take the folder to the new class.
- Grading will be as it has been in the past. Let me know if you need a rubric to grade this class. You should go over this rubric with your students.

Sample SSL Schedules: A Year at a Glance

September

Week One

Wednesday: SSR

Have students set up folders. Discuss the schedule for the week. Establish your rules and expectations for the class. Make sure you are enthusiastic about the class so the students will be, too! Allow them to read silently, time permitting.

Thursday: SSW

Writing Prompts:

- Today is your first week of seventh/eighth grade. What do you think this year will be like? What are your impressions of your classes? How will things be different from last year?
- What was your summer like? What did you do? Are you happy to be back at school?
- Student Choice

Friday: RA

Read the short story "Liverwurst and Roses" from *I Love You, I Hate You, Get Lost* by Ellen Conford, or have a student read aloud. Preview these and PRACTICE first!

Week Two

Monday: SSR

Pass out surveys. Have students fill these out, and place them in their folders. Discuss the survey—ask for volunteers to give their input about their feelings regarding reading and writing. Have students begin reading silently, time permitting.

Tuesday: SSR

Pass out Book Pass forms. Give each student one book. They get two to three minutes to look at the book (front cover, back cover, read the inside, etc.). On their book pass sheet, they write the title, author, and a comment (a narrative, or a grade, or a rating) on whether they think they would want to read the book. After two or three minutes, you say "pass," and they pass the book to the student to the right (or behind them). Repeat the process until each student has his or her first book back.

Discuss their favorites, different genres, and (possibly) how to identify the title and author. Start sustained silent reading, time permitting.

Wednesday: SSR

Have students read silently. You should be reading as well. Give them a minute or two to write in their logs at the end of class.

Thursday: SSW

Writing prompts:

- How do you feel about reading? What do you like to read? How often do you read? What is the purpose of reading?
- How do you feel about writing? What do you like to write? How often do you write?
- Student Choice

Friday: RA

Read the assorted poems by Sara Holbrook and Judith Viorst, or have a student read. Preview these and PRACTICE first!

If you would rather read an ongoing book to your students on Fridays, the books listed below are popular titles.

A Child Called "It" by Dave Pelzer
The Lost Boy by Dave Pelzer
Who Put That Hair in My Toothbrush? by Jerry Spinelli
Crash by Jerry Spinelli
Scorpions by Walter Dean Myers
Don't You Dare Read This, Mrs. Dunphrey by Margaret Haddix

Week Three

Monday–Wednesday: SSR

Promote SSR. Model reading yourself! Discuss what everyone is reading.

Thursday: SSW
Writing Prompts:
- Did your school last year have some sort of SSR (reading) program? What was it like? Do you think it helped you read better (or enjoy reading)?
- What is your most favorite and least favorite thing about school? Why?
- Student Choice

October

Week One
Monday–Wednesday: SSR

Thursday: SSW
Choose One:
- If you were given $5,000, but had to spend it in one store, where would you go and what would you buy?
- If you had to eat in one restaurant for the rest of your life, which one would you choose and why? If you had to eat just one meal, what would you order?
- Student Choice

Friday: RA
Read the article "O Romeo, O, Like, Wow" from *Columbus Dispatch,* or have a student read. Practice first.

Week Two:
Monday–Wednesday: SSR

Thursday: SSW
Choose One:
- When did you last cry? Why? Were you by yourself? In front of someone?
- What do you value most in a friend? What makes a good friend? What ruins a friendship?
- Student Choice

Friday: RA
Read the excerpt from *Nightmare Hall: The Silent Scream* by Diane Hoh, or have a student read aloud. Practice first! This might be a scary one to some of the students. You need to preview it!

Week Three
Monday–Wednesday: SSR

Thursday: SSW
Choose One:

- If you could take a one-month trip anywhere in the world, and money was not a consideration, where would you go and what would you do? Who would you take with you?
- If you were at a friend's house for a special dinner (like Thanksgiving), and you found a dead cockroach in your salad, what would you do? What if you were at a relative's house?
- Student Choice

Friday: RA
Read the excerpt from *On the Devil's Court* by Carl Deuker, or have a student read aloud. Practice first.

Week Four
Monday–Wednesday: SSR

Thursday: SSW
Choose One:
- Do you think professional athletes get paid too much money? Why or why not? Are there any professions where you think the workers are not paid enough? Which ones?
- If you had to contribute three things to a time capsule that would be opened in a hundred years, what three things would you choose to represent your generation? Why?
- Student Choice

Friday: RA
Read the following excerpt from Jerry Spinelli's *Maniac Magee,* or have a student read aloud. Practice first.

The read-aloud selections are often not complete stories, but excerpts. They are meant to make the students want to read the book. If you have extra time after reading the selection, ask for questions or predictions. Ask students if they have read anything similar to that story. Or, use one of the books suggested in the September packet and read one book continually each Friday.

November

Week One
Monday–Wednesday: SSR
Promote SSR. Model reading. Share books (book talk).

Thursday: SSW
Choose One:
- At what age should kids be allowed to wear whatever they want to school? Why? Should there ever be a dress code/uniform? Why or why not?

- At what age should kids be allowed to date? Why?
- Student Choice

Friday: RA
Read the excerpt from *Running Loose* by Chris Crutcher or have a student read aloud.

Week Two
Monday–Wednesday: SSR

Thursday: SSW
Choose One:
- Why do you think the most popular kids in school are so popular? In what ways do you think you are better than they are?
- Do you try to act like your friends more, or do they try to act like you? Why?
- Student Choice

Friday: RA
Read the excerpt from *Weasel* by Cynthia DeFelice or have a student read aloud.

Week Three: Thanksgiving Break

Week Four
Monday–Wednesday: SSR

Thursday: SSW
Choose One:
- Do you usually say what you really think, or what you believe people want to hear? Why?
- What things that you were afraid of a few years ago no longer bother you now? Why do you think you no longer feel that fear?
- Student Choice.

Friday: RA
Read the excerpt from *Slam!* by Walter Dean Myers or have a student read aloud.

December

Week One
Friday: RA was on your November schedule.

Week Two
Monday–Wednesday: SSR

Thursday: SSW
Choose One:
- Would you be willing to have horrible nightmares every night for a year if at the end of it all you would be a millionaire?
- Are there people that you envy enough that you would want to trade lives with them? Who are they and why do you envy them?
- Student Choice

Friday: No RA: Parent Conference Day

Week Three
Monday–Wednesday: SSR

Thursday: SSW
Choose One:
- Would you be willing to become extremely ugly physically if it meant that you could live for 1,000 years at any physical age you chose? Why or why not?
- If, at birth, you could select the profession your child would pursue, would you do so? Would you want your parents to have had the ability to choose your future profession? Why or why not?
- Student Choice

Friday: RA
Read (or have a student read) the attached story "My Most Memorable Christmas" from *Chicken Soup for the Teenage Soul II*. Practice first!
HAPPY HOLIDAYS!!!

January

Week One
Monday–Wednesday: SSR

Thursday: SSW
Choose One:
- Do you remember being read to as a child? What did your parents read to you? What is your favorite story?
- What is the best thing you did over the holiday break? Why was it the best?
- Student Choice

Friday: RA
Read the attached short story, "Moon Over Missouri," from Donald Gallo's *No Easy Answers,* or have a student read aloud. Preview and practice first!

Week Two
Monday–Wednesday: SSR

Thursday: SSW

Choose One:

- Would you rather be a rich and famous movie star or a doctor who saves a lot of people, but who is not wealthy or well known? Why?
- Of all the nice things someone could truthfully say about you, which one would make you feel the best? Why?
- Student Choice

Friday: RA

Read (or have a student read) the attached story "The All-American Slurp" from Donald Gallo's *Visions*. Practice first!

Week Three

Monday–Wednesday: SSR

Thursday: SSW

Choose One:

- The schoolwide spelling bee is coming up. Do you wish you were in it? Why or why not?
- What is one of your most embarrassing moments? What happened? Do you embarrass easily?
- Student Choice

Friday: RA

Read the excerpt from *Twice Taken* by Susan Beth Pfeffer or have a student read. Practice and preview first.

Week Four

Monday–Wednesday: SSR

Thursday: SSW

Choose One:

- If you could have anyone you know as a best friend, who would you pick and why? Are you friends with this person now? Why or why not?
- What do you choose in a game or truth and dare—truth or dare? Why? Do you ever pick the other? When and why?
- Student Choice

Friday: RA

Read the excerpt from Jerry Spinelli's *Wringer*, or have a student read. Practice first!

February

Teachers: So far for the second trimester, students should have eighteen reading entries (one was a fire drill on 12/12) and seven writing entries.

Idea!: Introduce novels by African American authors (or novels about African Americans) in honor of Black History Month. Suggested authors are Langston Hughes, Maya Angelou, Alice Walker, Toni Morrison, Christopher Paul Curtis, Mildred Taylor, Walter Dean Myers, Richard Wright, Martin Luther King, Jr., Terry McMillan, and so on.

Week One

Monday–Wednesday: SSR

Thursday: SSW

Choose One:

- How many important/influential African Americans (in history, through today) can you name? (Think about education, history, entertainment, arts, sports, etc.) What are/were their contributions to society?
- Think about your own hopes for the future. Write your own mini-version of Martin Luther King, Jr.'s "I Have a Dream" speech.
- Student Choice

Friday: RA

For a glimpse of race relations between 1920 and 1950, read the attached excerpt from *Roll of Thunder, Hear My Cry* by Mildred Taylor, or have a student read aloud. Practice first!

Week Two

Monday–Wednesday: SSR

Thursday: SSW

Choose One:

- How was your Valentine's Day yesterday? Did you purchase a data match sheet? Why or why not? Were you surprised at the person with whom you were paired?
- There is a saying that "love conquers all." Do you believe in this? Why or why not?
- Student Choice

Friday: RA

Read the attached story (an excerpt from *Stargirl* by Jerry Spinelli) or have a student read aloud.

Week Three

Monday–Wednesday: SSR

Thursday: SSW

Choose One:

- What place is your team in the spirit competition? What could you do to improve?

- Are you a "thinker" or a "doer"? What makes you that way? Do you like that you are that way?
- Student Choice

Friday: RA
Read the attached stories about Abraham Lincoln and Charles Schultz from *Chicken Soup for the Teenage Soul*, or have a student read aloud.

March

Week One
Monday–Wednesday: SSR

Thursday: SSW
Choose One:
- Do you know whose birthday is tomorrow? Do you think Dr. Seuss made important contributions to society? Why or why not? How many books by him can you name? Did you read them as a child?
- How many minutes/hours do you think you read a day (at home and at school)? Is it enough? Why or why not? Studies show that the average eighth grader should be reading 25 minutes every day in school and 20 minutes at night four times per week to improve reading and vocabulary.
- Student Choice

Encourage students to attend the speech tournament—tonight, 7 P.M.

Friday: RA
Today is the official birthday of Dr. Seuss. We will celebrate it on Tuesday, March 2. You will receive a memo from Ms. Hemmelgarn asking you for guest readers. Please prepare those students by letting them practice their chosen selections. For today's reading selection, why not read a Dr. Seuss book? Or read the attached poem "A Prayer for the Children."

Week Two
Monday–Wednesday: SSR

Thursday: SSW
Choose One:
- When you are striving for something you really want, and you don't get it, do you often quit, or keep trying? What makes you give up? What makes you keep trying?
- Do you see yourself running for public office one day? Why or why not? If you were elected president, what is the first thing you would do?
- Student Choice

Friday: RA
Read the attached excerpt from *The Giver* by Lois Lowry, or have a student read aloud.

Week Three
Monday–Wednesday: SSR

Thursday: SSW
Choose One:
- If you had only five minutes to think up a nickname for yourself, and you knew you would be called by it for the rest of your life, what would you choose? Why? What would you pick for your best friend? Your parents?
- Imagine that the principal told you she wanted to make the school even better, and would change it in any way you suggested. What would you tell her to do? Why?
- Student Choice

Friday: RA
Read the attached newspaper article from the *Los Angeles Times* about Tookie, cofounder of the gang the Crips.

Week Four
Monday–Wednesday: SSR

Thursday: SSW
Choose One:
- If your parents come to conference day, what are you hoping they will hear about you? Will it be accurate? What will you say to them about it?
- What will you do tomorrow if you do not come to school? Will you come to Parent Conference Day with your parents? Why or why not?
- Student Choice

Friday: No RA: Parent Conference Day

Week Five
Monday–Wednesday: SSR

Thursday: SSW
Choose One:
- When was the last time you were generous to a stranger just because you wanted to be nice? What did you do?
- When was the last time you took your anger out on someone else? Why did you do that? What happened?
- Student Choice

Friday: RA
Read the attached excerpt from *The Watsons Go to Birmingham—1963* by
Christopher Paul Curtis, or have a student read aloud. Practice first.

April

Start promoting our "Look Who's Reading" campaign. There have been
announcements encouraging students to read each morning. If you know of
a student who is in the process of finishing or has finished a great book, ask
him or her to fill out the attached book review. (You will need to make
copies, as necessary.) Submit the book review to Mr. Roles. He, along with
ASB, will choose book reviews to highlight on our hallway bulletin boards.
If your student's review is selected, he or she will get a picture taken, which
will also be displayed on the bulletin board. We want students to see and
hear about all of the students and adults who are reading! Feel free to submit
your own book review also!

Week One
Monday–Wednesday: SSR

Thursday: SSW
Choose One:
- Are you more likely to hold back your tears when you feel like crying,
  or hold back laughter when something is funny? Why?
- Do you wish your parents would question you more or less about what
  you do and how you feel? Why?
- Student Choice

Friday: RA
Read the attached excerpt or have a student read, but practice first. It is
called "Heading Home" and I think I got it from *Read* magazine. If you stop
at the dotted lines, and ask for predictions, it works well. Caution—the ending is a little gory! If you have time, discuss the use of the word
reMEMBERing (line E).

Week Two
Monday–Wednesday: SSR

Thursday: SSW
Choose One:
- If you could change any one thing about the way you look, what would
  you change? Why?
- Are you afraid to ask questions when you don't understand something?
  Do you ever fake a laugh when you don't get a joke? Why?
- Student Choice

Friday: RA
Read the attached poem "Making Sarah Cry" from *Chicken Soup for the Teenage Soul* or have a student read. Practice first!

Week Three: Spring Break

Week Four
Monday–Wednesday: SSR

Thursday: SSW
Choose One:
- ■ If you were to be granted any one magical power, what would you pick and why?
- ■ If you could be either the most attractive, smartest, most athletic, or the most liked kid in your grade, which would you choose and why?
- ■ Student Choice

Friday: RA
Read the attached excerpt from Edward Bloor's *Tangerine*, or have a student read aloud. Practice first!

Book Review

Name: _____ Grade: ___ Team: ___ SSL#___
The book I am reading is _____
by _____ .
It is about (DON'T GIVE AWAY THE ENDING) _____
_____ .
I would recommend it to a friend (tell why) because _____
_____ .
The best book I have EVER read is _____ .
I recommend it because _____
_____ .

You may make a copy of the front cover of the book, or draw it here:

May

Week One: SAT-9 Testing: No SSL

Week Two
Monday–Wednesday: SSR
Promote SSR. Model reading. Share books. Give book talks!

Thursday: SSW
Choose One:

- How do you think you did on the SAT-9¿ What could you have done better to prepare¿
- Do you think grades or test scores are more important¿ Why¿
- Student Choice

Friday: RA
Read the story "Loving Yourself First" from *Chicken Soup for the Teenage Soul III.*

Week Three
Monday–Wednesday: SSR

Thursday: SSW
Choose One:
- If you could make a TV show about anything you wanted, and you knew that millions of people would see it, what would it be about¿
- What do you think your friends like most about you¿ If you lost that quality, do you think they would still like you¿ Why or why not¿
- Student Choice

Friday: RA
Read the excerpt from *The Lost Boy* by Dave Pelzer or have a student read aloud.

David Pelzer is the author of four unbelievable books: *A Child Called "It," The Lost Boy, A Man Named Dave* and *Help Yourself.* They are true stories of the child abuse he endured from his mother until he was removed from the home at age twelve. There are a few teachers who are reading the books aloud to SSL classes on Friday—and the students are completely engrossed!

Dave Pelzer now travels as a speaker (to businesses as well as schools). I think it would be phenomenal if we could get him to come here! He is completely booked for the year 2000, but we may be able to get him in 2001. I have information on his rates and speech topics. Let me know if you are interested!

June

Week One
Monday–Wednesday: SSR

Thursday: SSW
Choose One:
- How do you feel about Olympic Day¿ Did you enjoy it¿ Did you compete¿
- If you could go to any school next year, where would you want to go and why¿
- Student Choice

Friday: RA
Read the excerpt from *Standing Up to Mr. O* by Claudia Mills, or have a student read aloud.

Week Two
Monday–Wednesday: SSR

Thursday: No SSW: Knotts Berry Farm Trip

Friday: RA
Read the attached excerpt from *The Skin I'm In* by Sharon Flake, or have a student read aloud. Practice first!

Surveys

Teachers: I am collecting data on our SSL program. Please fill out the attached teacher survey. Also, if you have the opportunity, please read the student survey aloud; tally the number of responses you receive and place in my mailbox! THANK YOU!

Have a wonderful summer!

Titles for Teens

Favorite Young Adult Literature Titles

Anderson, Laurie	*Speak	Abuse
Anonymous	**Go Ask Alice	Drug dependency
Avi	Nothing but the Truth	Standing up for oneself
	Wolf Rider	Murder/pranks
Bauer, Joan	Rules of the Road	Comedy/high school
Bauer, Marion	On My Honor	Swimming accident
Bloor, Edward	Tangerine	Soccer/handicap
Byars, Betsy	The Pinballs	Foster homes
Canfield, Jack	Chicken Soup for the Soul (series)	Nonfiction stories
	Chicken Soup for the Teenage Soul (series)	Advice
	Chicken Soup for the Preteen Soul	Advice
Catling, Patrick	The Chocolate Touch	Greed/lust for chocolate
Cisneros, Sandra	The House on Mango Street	Spanish-speaking Chicago
Cleary, Beverly	Dear Mr. Henshaw	Authors/divorce
Clements, Andrew	Frindle	Creative vocabulary
Codnum, Michael	*Rundown	Sibling jealousy
Coman, Carolyn	What Jamie Saw	Child abuse
Cooney, Caroline	*Driver's Ed	Accidental death
	Face on the Milk Carton	Missing child
	Whatever Happened to Janie?	Life after kidnapping
	The Voice on the Radio	Life after kidnapping
Cormier, Robert	*The Chocolate War	Candy sales/conformity
	*Beyond the Chocolate War	Conformity
	*Heroes	World War II
Coville, Bruce	The Monster's Ring	Jekyll-and-Hyde-type
Crutcher, Chris	*The Crazy Horse Electric Game	Sports/injury
	*Chinese Handcuffs	Sports/injury
	*Ironman	Sports/injury

	Running Loose	Sports/injury
	Staying Fat for Sarah Byrnes	Sports/abuse
	Stotan!	Sports/abuse
	Whale Talk	Sports/prejudice
Curtis, Christopher Paul	*The Watsons Go to Birmingham—1963*	Civil rights/family
	Bud, Not Buddy	Foster home
Cushman, Karen	*The Midwife's Apprentice*	Medieval
Cusick, Richie	*Teacher's Pet*	Thriller
Dahl, Roald	*Charlie and the Chocolate Factory*	Fantasy
	James and the Giant Peach	Fantasy
Danziger, Paula	*Can You Sue Your Parents for Malpractice?*	Teen's legal rights
	The Cat Ate My Gymsuit	Growing up
	Divorce Express	Divorce
	PS Longer Letter Later	Long distance friendship
DeFelice, Cynthia	*Weasel*	Frontier 1800
DiCamillo, Kate	*Because of Winn-Dixie*	Child/dog relationship
	The Tiger Rising	Friendship/truth
Draper, Sharon	*Darkness Before Dawn*	Teen relationship
	Forged by Fire	Drinking/driving
	Tears of a Tiger	Basketball/alcohol
Duncan, Lois	*I Know What You Did Last Summer*	Drinking/driving
	Killing Mr. Griffin	Abuse of teacher
Ewing, Lynne	*Drive-By*	Gangs/drive-by shootings
	Party Girl	Teens/alcohol
Flake, Sharon	*The Skin I'm In*	Tolerance
Fleischman, Paul	*Whirligig*	Death/responsibility
Fleischman, Sid	*The Whipping Boy*	Orphans/abduction
Freller, James	*Rock Solid*	Wrestling
Gantos, Jack	*Jack's Black Book*	Pets/death
	Joey Pigza Loses Control	ADHD/parental relationships
	Joey Pigza Swallowed a Key	ADHD
Garcia, Rita Williams	*Like Sisters on the Homefront*	Teen pregnancy
Grimes, Nikki	*Jazmin's Notebook*	Life in Harlem
Haddix, Margaret	*Among the Hidden*	Government control
	Don't You Dare Read This, Mrs. Dunphrey	Abandonment
	Just Ella	Cinderella spoof
Hayden, Torey	*Tiger's Child*	Special education
	One Child	Special education
Hesse, Karen	*Letters from Rifka*	Holocaust
	Out of the Dust	Oklahoma dust bowl
Hinojosa, Maria	*Crews: Gang Members Talk*	Gangs
Hinton, S. E.	*The Outsiders*	Gangs
	Tex	Coming of age

	Rumblefish	Teen fighting
	That Was Then, This Is Now	Drugs
Howe, James	*The Watcher*	Death
Hunt, Irene	*The Lottery Rose*	Abuse
	No Promises in the Wind	The Depression/1932
Jordan, Michael	*I Can't Accept Not Trying*	Motivational
Klass, David	*Danger Zone*	Basketball
Korman, Gordon	*No More Dead Dogs*	Teenage rebillion
	The Sixth Grade Nickname Game	Nicknames
Krisher, Trudy	*Spite Fences*	Prejudice
Lee, Milly	*Nim and the War Effort*	Chinatown/World War II
Levine, Michael	*The Kid's Address Book*	Letter writing
Lowry, Lois	*The Giver*	Futuristic
	Number the Stars	Holocaust
Macaulay, David	*The Way Things Work*	How things work
	The New Way Things Work	How things work
Many, Paul	*These Are the Rules*	Male coming-of-age
Mazer, Norma Fox	*Silver*	Popularity/abuse
Mills, Claudia	*Standing Up to Mr. O*	Dissection/biology
Minsky, Ruth	*The Cage*	Holocaust
Moore, Martha	*Under the Mermaid Angel*	Adoption
Myers, Walter Dean	*Bad Boy*	Autobiography
	Hoops	Basketball
	Slam!	Basketball vs. academics
	Monster	Gangs/robbery
	Scorpions	Gangs
Newman, L.	*Fat Chance*	Bulimia
O'Brien, Robert	*Z for Zachariah*	Science fiction
Orr, Wendy	*Peeling the Onion*	Tragic car accident
Park, Barbara	*Mick Harte Was Here*	Death/helmet laws
	Skinnybones	Small boy/big mouth
Paterson, Katherine	*The Great Gilly Hopkins*	Foster care
Patrick, James	*Meet the Stars of Professional Wrestling*	Wrestling
Paulsen, Gary	*The Car*	Coming of age
	The Cookcamp	Wilderness/World War II
	Hatchet	Survival
	The Rifle	Revolutionary War
	The Winter Room	1930s farm life
Pearson, Mary	*David V. God*	Fear of dying/heaven
Peck, Robert Newton	*A Day No Pigs Would Die*	Death/family
	Soup	Humor
Pelzer, Dave	*A Child Called "It"*	Child abuse
	The Lost Boy	Child abuse
	A Man Named Dave	Child abuse
	Help Yourself	

Peters, Julie Anne	*Define "Normal"*	Unlikely friendship
Pfeffer, Susan	*Twice Taken*	Missing children
Philbrick, Rodman	*Freak the Mighty*	Special education/ friendship
	Max the Mighty	Child abuse/runaways
	The Last Book in the Universe	Science fiction
Quarles, Heather	*A Door Near Here*	Abandonment
Raskin, Ellen	*The Westing Game*	Mystery
Rawls, Wilson	*Where the Red Fern Grows*	Pets/death
Sachar, Louis	*Holes*	Juvenile detention
Scieszka, Jon	*Knights of the Kitchen Table*	Camelot/King Arthur
Sebestyen, Ouida	*Girl in the Box*	Kidnapping
	Word by Heart	Prejudice
Soto, Gary	*Buried Onions*	Life in Fresno
Sparks, Beatrice	**Annie's Baby*	Teen pregnancy
	**It Happened to Nancy*	Date rape/AIDS
	**Jay's Journal*	Cults
	**Treacherous Love*	Teacher/student relationship
Spinelli, Jerry	*Maniac Magee*	Racism/friendship
	Who Put That Hair in My Toothbrush?	Sibling relationships
	Wringer	Pigeon hunting
	The Library Card	Short stories
Stine, R. L.	*Bad Dreams*	Mystery
Stock, Gregory	*The Book of Questions*	Mature content
	The Kids' Book of Questions	Great for writing prompts
Sykes, Shelley	*For Mike*	Suspense/kidnapping
Tashjian, Janet	*Multiple Choice*	Compulsive behavior
Taylor, Mildred	*The Friendship*	Friendship
	Roll of Thunder, Hear My Cry	Racism/1930s
Tillage, Leon Walter	*Leon's Story*	Segregation
Trueman, Terry	*Stuck in Neutral*	Cerebral palsy
Voigt, Cynthia	*Dicey's Song*	Family
	Izzy Willy Nilly	Drinking/loss of a limb
	The Runner	Family struggles
Wallace, Rich	*Wrestling Sturbridge*	Wrestling
White, Ruth	*Belle Prater's Boy*	Mystery/death
Wynne-Jones, Tim	*The Book of Changes*	Humor/coming of age
Yolen, Jane	*The Devil's Arithmetic*	Holocaust
Zindel, Paul	*The Pigman*	Teens and the elderly

*Contains mature content
**High school readers only

Books in a Series

Elfman, Eric	The X-Files
Golden, Chris	Buffy, The Vampire Slayer
Gutman, Bill	Millbrook Sports
Lanham, Cheryl	Life at Sixteen
Lewis, C. S.	Chronicles of Narnia
Metz, Melinda	Roswell High
Pascal, Francine	Sweet Valley High
	Sweet Valley University
Paulsen, Gary	World of Adventure
Pike, Christopher	The Last Vampire
Rees, Elizabeth	Heart Beats
Schwemm, Diane	The Year I Turned Sixteen
Stine, R. L.	The Cheerleader
	Fear Park
	Fear Street
	Fear Street Sagas
	Goosebumps
	Super Chiller Series

Series by Various Authors

(Listed by publisher)

Pocket Books	Clueless
	Dawson's Creek Series
Scholastic	Dear America
Simon & Schuster	Star Trek: Deep Space Nine
	Star Trek: The Next Generation

Content Area Titles

Social Studies/History

Aliki	*A Medieval Feast*	Medieval
Ancona, George	*Powwow*	Native Americans
Aron, Paul	*Unsolved Mysteries of American History: An Eye-Opening Journey Through 500 Years of Discoveries, Disappearances, and Baffling Events*	American history
Bitton-Jackson, L.	*I Have Lived a Thousand Lives: Growing Up in the Holocaust*	Holocaust

Beals, Melba	*Warriors Don't Cry*	Integration/diary
Bernall, Misty	*She Said Yes: The Unlikely Martydom of Cassie Bernall*	Columbine
Biesty, Stephen	*Incredible Cross-Sections*	Interior designs
Booth, David	*The Dust Bowl*	Oklahoma
Chang, Ina	*A Separate Battle: Women and the Civil War*	Civil War
Clinton, C.	*Scholastic's Encyclopedia of the Civil War*	Civil War
Coerr, Eleanor	*Sadako and the Thousand Paper Cranes*	Radiation
Collier, James	*My Brother Sam Is Dead*	Revolutionary War
Cushman, Karen	*Catherine, Called Birdie*	Medieval
Filipovic, Zlata	*Zlata's Diary: A Child's Life in Sarajevo*	Sarajevo
Fox, Paula	*The Slave Dancer*	Pre–Civil War
Freedman, Russell	*Indian Chiefs*	Indian life
	Lincoln: A Photobiography	Abraham Lincoln
Fry, Somerset	*History of the World*	World history
Gibbons, Gail	*Knights in Shining Armor*	Medieval
Glicksman, Jane	*Cool Geography: Miles of Maps, Wild Adventures, Fun Activities, Facts from Around the World, and More*	Geography
Greenwood, B.	*The Last Safe House: A Story of the Underground Railroad*	Slavery
Hamilton, Virginia	*Many Thousand Games: African Americans from Slavery to Freedom*	Slavery
Hunt, Irene	*Across Five Aprils*	Civil War
Lowry, Lois	*The Giver*	Futuristic
Miles, Lisa	*The Usborne Illustrated Atlas of World History*	World history
Myers, Walter Dean	*Malcolm X*	Civil rights
Nelson, Pam	*Cool Women: The Thinking Girl's Guide to the Hippest Women in History*	Women in history
Paterson, Katherine	*Jacob I Have Loved*	Maine—World War II
Peck, Robert Newton	*A Day No Pigs Would Die*	1920s
Polacco, Patricia	*The Keeping Quilt*	Family history
	Pink and Say	Civil War
Scieszka, Jon	*Knights of the Kitchen Table*	King Arthur
	The Good, the Bad, and the Goofy	Wild West
	It's All Greek to Me	Greek life
Stanley, Jerry	*Children of the Dust Bowl*	Depression
Taylor, Mildred	*Roll of Thunder, Hear My Cry*	1930s
Time Magazine	*Bridges and Borders: Diversity in America*	American history
Yep, Lawrence	*Dragonwings*	Chinese immigration

Science

Allen, Judy	*Are You a Snail?*	Animal life
Arnold, Nick	Horrible Science Series	Various science topics
Arnosky, Jim	*All About Rattlesnakes*	Snakes
Barton, Byron	*I Want to Be an Astronaut*	Air travel
Bond, Nancy	*The Voyage Begun*	Depletion energy
Caney, Steven	*The Invention Book*	Inventions
Engdahl, Sylvia	*The Far Side of Evil*	Nuclear power
Farmer, Penelope	*The Ear, the Eye, and the Arm*	Genes
George, Jean	*Julie*	Science/tundra
	Julie of the Wolves	Survival
	The Cry of the Crow	Pets/family
Hesse, Karen	*Phoenix Rising*	Contamination
Jones, Charlotte	*Mistakes That Worked*	Surprising inventions
Kumin, Maxine	*The Microscope*	Tools for science
Myers, Jack	*What Makes Popcorn Pop? And Other Questions About the World Around Us*	Interesting questions
Parsons, A.	*Amazing Snakes*	Snakes
Paulsen, Gary	*Dogsong*	Eskimo/survival
Pringle, Laurence	*Bats! Strange and Wonderful*	Bats
Sleator, William	*House of Stairs*	Psychological experiments
Trefil, James	*1001 Things Everyone Should Know About Science*	Interesting facts
Voorhees, Don	*Why Does Popcorn Pop? And 201 Other Fascinating Facts About Food*	Facts about food

Health/Physical Education

Blume, Judy	*Deenie*	Scoliosis
Byars, Betsy	*Cracker Jackson*	Spouse abuse
Coman, Carolyn	*What Jamie Saw*	Abuse
Conly, Jane	*Crazy Lady*	Mental handicap
Crutcher, Chris	*Athletic Shorts: Six Short Stories*	Sports/injury
	Ironman	Sports/injury
	Chinese Handcuffs	Sports/injury
	Staying Fat for Sarah Byrnes	Sports/abuse
	Running Loose	Sports/injury
	Stotan!	Sports/abuse
Draper, Sharon	*Tears of a Tiger*	Basketball/alcohol
	Forged by Fire	Death/family struggles
Fine, Anne	*Flour Babies*	Child rearing
Krull, Kathleen	*Wilma Unlimited: How Wilma Rudolph Became the World's Fastest Woman*	Polio/Olympic athlete

Lipsyte, Robert	*The Contender*	Drug abuse/Harlem
Littlefield, Bill	*Champions: Stories of Ten Remarkable Athletes*	Sports
Macy, Sue	*A Whole New Ball Game: The Story of the All-American Girls Professional Baseball League*	Girls' basketball
Mazer, Norma Fox	*After the Rain*	Aging/death
Nelson, Theresa	*Earthshine*	Parent with AIDS
Oneal, Zibby	*The Language of Goldfish*	Depression/suicide
Voight, Cynthia	*Dicey's Song*	Mental illness
	Homecoming	Abandonment/family

Mathematics

Blum, Raymond	*Mathemagic*
Enzensberger,H.	*The Number Devil*
Juster, Norton	*The Phantom Tollbooth*
Lasky, Kathryn	*The Librarian Who Measured the Earth*
Sachar, Louis	*Sideways Arithmetic from Wayside School*
Scieszka, Jon	*The Math Curse*

Fine Arts

| Adams, Ansel | *The Portfolios of Ansel Adams* |
| Van Allsburg, Chris | *The Mysteries of Harris Burdick* |

Favorite Read-Aloud Selections

Bauer, Marion	*On My Honor*	Pages 27–29
Bethancourt, Ernesto	"Moon Over Missouri" in *No Easy Answers,* ed. Don Gallo	
Bloor, Edward	*Tangerine*	Pages 1–4
Burch, Bruce	"The Premonition" in *Chicken Soup for the Soul,* ed. Jack Canfield	
Cisneros, Sandra	"Eleven" in *Chicken Soup for the Teenage Soul,* ed. Jack Canfield	
Cochran, Thomas	*Roughnecks*	Pages 3–9
Coman, Carolyn	*What Jamie Saw*	Chapter 1
Crutcher, Chris	*Whale Talk*	Pages 22–24
Curtis, Christopher Paul	*Bud, Not Buddy*	Chapter 6
	The Watsons Go to Birmingham—1963	Pages 1–5

DiCamillo, Kate	*Because of Winn-Dixie*	Chapter 3
Draper, Sharon	*Tears of a Tiger*	Pages 1–10
Duane, Diane	"Midnight Snack" in *Sixteen,* ed. Don Gallo	
Ewing, Lynne	*Drive-By*	Chapter 1
Flake, Sharon	*The Skin I'm In*	Chapter 1
Florian, Douglas	"Mr. Backward" in *Bing Bang Boing*	
Fulghum, Richard	*All I Really Need to Know I Learned in Kindergarten*	Pages 3–6
Gantos, Jack	*Joey Pigza Loses Control*	Pages 1–6
	Joey Pigza Swallowed a Key	Pages 1–5
Gorog, Judith	"Doglicks" and "The Snooping Sitter" in *When Nobody's Home: Fifteen Babysitting Tales of Terror*	
Haddix, Margaret	*Don't You Dare Read This, Mrs. Dunphrey*	Chapter 1
Harden, Mike	"O Romeo, O, Like, Wow," *Columbus Dispatch,* November 8, 1989	
Hesse, Karen	*Out of the Dust*	Pages 3–15
Holbrook, Sara	"I Hate My Body" and "I Never Said I Wasn't Difficult" from *I Never Said I Wasn't Difficult*	
Holmes, Edward	"The Day of the Hunter" in *Maine Speaks: An Anthology of Maine Literature*	
Holt, Kimberly	*When Zachary Beaver Came to Town*	Chapter 1
Hughes, Langston	"Thank you Ma'am" in *Jump Up and Say! A Collection of Black Storytelling*	
Jennings, Paul	"A Mouthful" in *Uncovered! Weird, Weird Stories*	
Kerr, M. E.	"I've Got Gloria" in *No Easy Answers: Short Stories About Teenagers Making Tough Choices,* ed. Don Gallo	
Korman, Gordon	"A Reasonable Sum" in *Connections,* ed. Don Gallo	
Lowry, Lois	*The Giver*	Pages 1–4
Myers, Walter Dean	*Monster*	Chapter 1
	Scorpions	Chapter 1
Namioka, Lensey	"The All-American Slurp" in *Visions,* ed. Don Gallo	
Park, Barbara	*Mick Harte Was Here*	Chapter 1
Pearson, Mary	*David V. God*	Chapter 1
Peck, Richard	"Priscilla and the Wimps" in *Sixteen,* ed. Don Gallo	
Peck, Robert Newton	*A Day No Pigs Would Die*	Chapter 1
Pelzer, Dave	*A Child Called "It"*	Pages 3–8
	The Lost Boy	Pages 3–9
Philbrick, Rodman	*Freak the Mighty*	Chapter 1
	The Last Book in the Universe	Chapter 1
Quindlen, Anna	*A Short Guide to a Happy Life*	Pages 25–42
Sachar, Louis	*Holes*	Pages 5–7
Scieszka, Jon	*Knights of the Kitchen Table*	Chapter 1
Sebestyen, Ouida	*Girl in the Box*	Pages 4–15
Spinelli, Jerry	*Crash*	Chapter 1

	Maniac Magee	Pages 30–32 (Chapter 9)
	"School Spirit" in *Connections,* ed. Don Gallo	
	Stargirl	Pages 1–6
	Who Put That Hair in My Toothbrush?	Pages 36–41
	Wringer	Chapter 1
Strasser, Todd	"On the Bridge" in *Visions,* ed. Don Gallo	
Summey, Jason	"Be Cool . . . Stay in School" in *Chicken Soup for the Soul,* ed. Jack Canfield	
Vail, Rachel	*Do-Over*	Pages 1–4
Viorst, Judith	"If I Were in Charge of the World" in *If I Were in Charge of the World and Other Poems*	
Voight, Cynthia	*Izzy, Willy, Nilly*	Pages 1–5
Vry, Allen	"The Late Shift" in *Scary Stories for When You're Home Alone*	
Wynne-Jones, Tim	*The Book of Changes*	Pages 1–5
Yolen, Jane	*The Devil's Arithmetic*	Chapter 3
Zindel, Paul	*The Pigman*	Pages 1–3

Popular Audiobooks

Bauer, Marion	*On My Honor*
Blume, Judy	*Superfudge*
Byars, Betsy	*The Pinballs*
Christopher, Matt	*Baseball Pals*
Cleary, Beverly	*Dear Mr. Henshaw*
Crutcher, Chris	*Athletic Shorts*
	Ironman
	Stotan!
Curtis, Christopher Paul	*The Watsons go to Birmingham—1963*
Haddix, Margaret	*Don't You Dare Read This, Mrs. Dunphrey*
Hesse, Karen	*Out of the Dust*
Hinton, S. E.	*The Outsiders*
Hunt, Irene	*The Lottery Rose*
Lowry, Lois	*The Giver*
	Number the Stars
Myers, Walter Dean	*Scorpions*
Park, Barbara	*Mick Harte Was Here*
Paterson, Katherine	*The Bridge to Terabithia*
	The Great Gilly Hopkins
Paulsen, Gary	*Hatchet*
Rowling, J. K.	Harry Potter (series)

Sachar, Louis	*Holes*
Shreve, Susan	*The Flunking of Joshua T. Bates*
Spinelli, Jerry	*Crash*
	Who Put That Hair in my Toothbrush?
White, E. B.	*Charlotte's Web*
Yolen, Jane	*The Devil's Arithmetic*

Favorite Short Story Collections

Blume, Judy	*Places I Never Meant to Be: Original Stories by Censored Writers*
Canfield, Jack, ed.	*Chicken Soup for the Soul*
	A Second Helping of Chicken Soup for the Soul
	Chicken Soup for the Teenage Soul
	Chicken Soup for the Teenage Soul II
Clairday, Robynn	*Expect the Unexpected: Embarrassing Stories by Kids Just Like You*
Coville, Bruce	*Book of Monsters: Tales to Give You the Creeps*
Duncan, Lois	*Trapped! Cages of Mind and Body*
Gallo, Donald	*Connections: Short Stories by Outstanding Writers*
	Join In: Multiethnic Stories by Outstanding Writers
	No Easy Answers: Short Stories About Teenagers Making Tough Choices
	Sixteen: Short Stories by Outstanding Writers for Young Adults
	Short Circuits: Thirteen Shocking Stories by Outstanding Writers
	Time Capsule: Short Stories About Teenagers Throughout the Twentieth Century
	Ultimate Sports: Short Stories by Outstanding Writers
	Visions: Nineteen Short Stories by Outstanding Writers
Gorog, Judith	*When Nobody's Home: Fifteen Babysitting Tales of Terror*
Hamilton, Virginia	*Her Stories: African American Folktales, Fairy Tales, and True Tales*
	The People Could Fly: American Black Folktales
Jennings, Paul	*Listen Ear and Other Stories to Shock You Silly!*
	Uncovered! Weird, Weird Stories
	Unreal! Eight Surprising Stories
Monroe, Jack	*True Survival Stories*
Peck, Richard	*A Long Way from Chicago*
Schwartz, Alvin	*Scary Stories to Tell in the Dark*
	Scary Stories: More Tales to Chill Your Bones
Shapard, Robert	*Sudden Fiction: American Short Short Stories*
Sleator, T.	*Oddballs*
Soto, Gary	*Baseball in April and Other Stories*
Spinelli, Jerry	*The Library Card*
Stine, R. L.	*Nightmare Hour*
Welch, R. C.	*Scary Stories for Stormy Nights*

Wynne-Jones, Tim   *The Book of Changes*
Yep, Lawrence   *American Dragons: Twenty-Five Asian American Voices*
Yolen, Jane   *Twelve Short Stories About the Future*

Favorite Picture Books

Abnett, Dan   *Dinosaurs*
*Arnold, Ted   *No Jumping on the Bed*
Barrett, Judi   *Cloudy with a Chance of Meatballs*
Base, Graem   *Animalia*
*Blake, Quentin   *All Join In*
Bonson, Richard   *Disaster! Catastrophes That Shook the World*
*Brown, Margaret   *Goodnight Moon*
    The Important Book
*Brown, Ruth   *The Big Sneeze*
Bunting, Eve   *A Day's Work*
    The Wall
Butterfield, Moira   *1,000 Facts About the Earth*
Calmenson, S.   *The Principal's New Clothes*
Charlip, Remy   *Fortunately*
Davol, Marguerite   *How the Snake Got His Hiss*
*Downey, Lynn   *The Flea's Sneeze*
Florian, Douglas   *Beast Feast* (Illus. Poems)
George, Jean C.   *Everglades*
Green, Jen   *Desert Animals*
    Sea Creatures
Greenfield, Eloise   *For the Love of the Game: Michael Jordan and Me*
Heide, Florence   *The Shrinking of Treehorn*
Heller, Ruth   *Many Luscious Lollipops: A Book About Adjectives*
Herron, Carolivia   *Nappy Hair*
Hopkins, Andrea   *Romeo and Juliet*
*Janovitz, Marilyn   *Is It Time?*
King, Martin Luther, Jr.   *I Have a Dream*
Knowlton, Jack   *Geography from A to Z: A Picture Glossary*
Leedy, Loreen   *Postcards from Pluto: A Tour of the Solar System*
Levitt, Paul   *The Weighty Word Book*
Lindbergh, Reeve   *What Is the Sun?*
Mallory, Kenneth   *Families of the Deep Blue Sea*
Miller, William   *Richard Wright and the Library Card*
Paulos, Martha   *Insectasides*
Perry, Sarah   *If*
Polacco, Patricia   *Aunt Chip and the Great Triple Creek Affair*

	The Butterfly
	Pink and Say
	Thank You, Mr. Falker
Pope, Joyce	*Reptiles*
Rappaport, Doreen	*Freedom River*
Ringgold, Faith	*Aunt Harriet's Underground Railroad in the Sky*
Rosen, Michael	*A School for Pompey Walker*
San Souci, Robert	*The Samurai's Daughter*
Scieszka, Jon	*The Math Curse*
	The True Story of the Three Little Pigs
Sendak, Maurice	*Where the Wild Things Are*
Stidworthy, John	*Creepy Crawlies*
Tsuchiya, Yukio	*Faithful Elephants: A True Story of Animals, People, and War*
Van Allsburg, Chris	*The Wretched Stone*
Viorst, Judith	*Alexander and the Terrible, Horrible, No Good, Very Bad Day*
*Winter, Jeanette	*The House That Jack Built*
Wisniewski, David	*The Secret Knowledge of Grown-Ups*
*Wood, Audrey	*The Napping House*
Yolen, Jane	*Encounter*
Zimmerman, Howard	*Dinosaurs! The Biggest, Baddest, Strangest, Fastest*

*Contains rhyming patterns to support struggling readers

Wordless Picture Books

Blake, Quentin	*Clown*
Collington, Peter	*The Angel and the Soldier Boy*
	The Midnight Circus
dePaola, Tomie	*The Hunter and the Animals*
	Pancakes for Breakfast
Hutchins, Pat	*Changes, Changes*
Mayer, Mercer	*Frog Goes to Dinner*
	Frog on His Own
	Frog, Where Are You?
Popov, Nikolai	*Why?*
Rohmann, Eric	*Time Flies*
Spier, Peter	*Noah's Ark*
	Peter Spier's Christmas
Van Allsburg, Chris	*Ben's Dream*
Wiesner, David	*Sector 7*
	Tuesday

Magazines for Teens

Comics

Archie Comic Publications
Archie
Sabrina the Teenage Witch

Bongo Entertainment, Inc.
Simpsons

Dark Horse Comics
Star Wars Episode I

D. C. Comics
The Adventures of Superman
Batman
The Flintstones
The Jetsons
Robin

Marvel Comics
The Avengers
Captain America
X-Force

Content Area

Junior Scholastic (grades 6–8)
Scholastic Action (grades 7–12, reading levels 3–5)
Scholastic Art (grades 7–12)
Scholastic Choices (science and health, grades 7–12)

Scholastic Math (grades 6–9)
Scholastic Scope (language arts, grades 7–12)
Scholastic Update (social studies, grades 9–12)
Science World (grades 7–10)
Time Machine: The American History Magazine for Kids

Fashion/Popular Culture

American Girl
Biography
Entertainment Weekly
InStyle
Jane

Lucky
Movieline
People
Seventeen

Teen
Teen People
Us
YM

Motor Sports

Hot Rod

Sport Rider

Motorcross Action

Music

Bass
Guitar

New Music

Keyboard

News/Current Events

National Geographic Adventure
National Geographic
National Geographic World
News for You

Newsweek
Time
Time for Kids
U.S. News and World Report

Sports

Bicycling	*Sports Illustrated*
Cycle Sport	*Sports Illustrated for Kids*
Outdoor Life	*Wind Surfing*
Snowboarder	*WWF*
Soccer	

Poetry Collections

Angelou, Maya	*The Complete Collected Poems of Maya Angelou*
Bagert, Brod	*Let Me Be . . . the Boss: Poems for Kids to Perform*
Carlson, Lori	*Cool Salsa: Bilingual Poems on Growing Up*
Carroll, Lewis	*Jabberwocky*
Carson, Jo	*Stories I Ain't Told Nobody Yet*
Cole, William	*Poem Stew*
Dahl, Roald	*Dirty Beasts*
	Revolting Rhymes
Dakos, Kalli	*If You're Not Here, Please Raise Your Hand: Poems About School*
Dillard, Annie	*Mornings Like This: Found Poems*
Fleischman, Paul	*Joyful Noise*
Florian, Douglas	*Bing Bang Boing*
	Insectlopedia
	Laugh-eteria
Giovanni, Nikki	*The Selected Poems of Nikki Giovanni*
	Spin a Soft Black Song
Glenn, Mel	*Class Dismissed: High School Poems*
	Jump Ball: A Basketball Season in Poems
	The Taking of Room 114: A Hostage Drama in Poems
Graves, Donald	*Baseball, Snakes, and Summer Squash: Poems About Growing Up*
Greenfield, Eloise	*Honey, I Love, and Other Love Poems*
Harrison, Michael	*Splinters: A Book of Very Short Poems*
Holbrook, Sara	*Am I Naturally This Crazy?*
	Chicks Up Front
	The Dog Ate My Homework
	I Never Said I Wasn't Difficult
	Nothing's the End of the World
	Walking on the Boundaries of Change: Poems of Transition
Hopkins, Lee B.	*Marvelous Math: A Book of Poems*
	Side by Side: Poems to Read Together
	Extra Innings: Baseball Poems
Hudson, Wade	*Pass It On: African-American Poetry for Children*
Hughes, Langston	*The Dream Keeper and Other Poems*

Janeczko, Paul	*The Place My Words Are Looking For*
Lansky, Bruce	*Kids Pick the Funniest Poems*
Marsden, John	*Prayer for the Twenty-First Century*
Medearis, Angela S.	*Skin Deep and Other Teenage Reflections*
Myers, Walter Dean	*Harlem*
Nye, Naomi	*I Feel a Little Jumpy Around You*
Prelutsky, Jack	*The New Kid on the Block*
	The Random House Book of Poetry for Children
Silverstein, Shel	*A Light in the Attic*
	Where the Sidewalk Ends
Strickland, Michael	*Poems That Sing to You*
Viorst, Judith	*If I Were in Charge of the World and Other Worries*
Volavkova, Hana	*I Never Saw Another Butterfly*
Westcott, Nadine	*Never Take a Pig to Lunch: Poems About the Fun of Eating*

Resources for Teachers

Professional Resources

Reading/Writing Workshop

It's Never Too Late: Leading Adolescents to Lifelong Literacy by Janet Allen (Heinemann 1995). A teacher-researcher writes about helping at-risk high school students with a balanced literacy program in this great book.

There's Room for Me Here: Literacy Workshop in the Middle School by Janet Allen and Kyle Gonzalez (Stenhouse 1998). This is a fantastic example of how to set up and organize a literacy workshop classroom in your school. It details the literacy project in Kyle's middle school and contains great ready-to-use pages in the appendix.

In the Middle: Writing, Reading, and Learning with Adolescents by Nancie Atwell (Heinemann-Boynton/Cook 1987). This teacher-researcher book tells how to run a reading/writing workshop classroom.

Why Workshop? Changing Course in 7–12 English, edited by Richard Bullock (Stenhouse 1998). English teachers of grades 7–12 share stories and explain strategies for workshops in this book.

Reading and the Middle School Student by Judith Irvin (Allyn & Bacon 1997). This book shows how to help students learn how to read in a workshop-type classroom. There are also strategies and examples on how to teach reading across the curriculum.

Just Teach Me, Mrs. K by Mary Krogness (Heinemann 1995). This book shows how to help students learn in a workshop-type classroom, including some great ideas on how to incorporate drama and readers theater.

The Read-Aloud Handbook by Jim Trelease (Penguin 1993). This handbook is an excellent source for read-aloud selections, young adult literature titles, and poetry collections for all grades.

Reading

Yellow Brick Roads: Shared and Guided Paths to Independent Reading 4–12 by Janet Allen (Stenhouse 2000). This is a wonderful resource for learning how to implement independent, guided, and shared reading in your classroom.

Questioning the Author by Isabel L. Beck, Margaret G. McKeown, and Rebecca L. Hamilton (International Reading Association 1997). This book discusses specific strategies for getting students to interact with the text.

Into Focus: Understanding and Creating Middle School Readers by Kylene Beers and Barbara Samuels (Christopher-Gordon 1996). Linda Rief has written a powerful foreword to this book about middle school readers.

Tell Me: Children, Reading, and Talk by Aidan Chambers (Stenhouse 1996). This book shows you how to engage students in talking and listening well. The goal is to help children learn to clarify ideas for themselves and then communicate effectively with others.

Literature Circles: Voice and Choice in Book Clubs and Reading Groups, 2d ed., by Harvey Daniels (Stenhouse 2002). This book shows you how to model, set up, and conduct literature circles in your classroom.

Strategies That Work: Teaching Comprehension to Enhance Understanding by Stephanie Harvey and Anne Goudvis (Stenhouse 2000). Harvey and Goudvis have put together a good resource for teachers of middle and high school.

Reluctant Readers: Connecting Students and Books for Successful Reading Experiences by Ron Jobe and Mary Dayton-Sakari (Stenhouse 1999). Research and strategies are offered on how to connect students and books for successful reading.

Mosaic of Thought: Teaching Comprehension in a Reader's Workshop by Ellin Oliver Keene and Susan Zimmermann (Heinemann 1997). This contains theory and research on teaching comprehension in a reader's workshop. There is a great foreword by Donald Graves.

Reading To, With, and By Children by Margaret Mooney (Richard C. Owen 1990). This book offers research and strategies on the three types of reading students need to be exposed to daily.

The SSR Handbook: How to Organize and Manage a Sustained Silent Reading Program by Janice Pilgreen (Heinemann 2000). This book gives the research and theory behind SSR. Many studies are documented that make great arguments for starting an SSR program.

Supporting Intermediate and Secondary Readers by Armin R. Schulz (California Reading Association 1998). This small workbook explores interactive approaches for grades 4–12.

I Read It, but I Don't Get It: Comprehension Strategies for Adolescent Readers by Cris Tovani (Stenhouse 2000). This is an excellent, engaging book with ready-to-use coding sheets.

Sketching Stories, Stretching Minds: Responding Visually to Literature by Phyllis Whitin (Heinemann 1996). Whitin gives research and strategies for helping students visualize (or create mental pictures) while reading and writing.

Graphic Organizers and Mini-Lessons

50 Graphic Organizers for Reading, Writing, and More by Karen Bromley (Scholastic Professional Book Division 1999). This is very user-friendly and includes ready-to-copy graphic organizers such as the "data chart," "finding the main idea," "Venn diagrams," and more.

Gracious Gifts: A Glimpse at Selected Literary Jewels of the 1990s by Armin R. Schulz (California Reading Association 1997). This book is a big bibliography of popular titles of the 1990s, including poetry and nonfiction.

Nonfiction

Nonfiction Matters: Reading, Writing, and Research in Grades 3–8 by Stephanie Harvey (Stenhouse 1998). This is a great book for all content areas to help teach students reading, writing, and researching through nonfiction.

Vocabulary

Words, Words, Words: Teaching Vocabulary in Grades 4–12 by Janet Allen (Stenhouse 1999). This is a fantastic resource for teaching vocabulary. It includes an invaluable section on graphic organizers and other usable sheets.

Classrooms That Work by Richard Allington and Patricia Cunningham (Addison-Wesley 1998). A study in teaching language arts that includes ideas for word walls, sentence strips, graphic organizers, and how to set up your classroom (at both the elementary and middle school level).

Word Matters: Teaching Phonics and Spelling in the Reading/Writing Classroom by Gay Su Pinnell and Irene C. Fountas (Heinemann 1998). This is a companion to *Guided Reading* by Irene C. Fountas and Gay Su Pinnell (Heinemann 1996).

Writing

Craft Lessons: Teaching Writing K–8 by Ralph Fletcher and JoAnn Portalupi (Stenhouse 1998). This is a very well-organized book on how to teach writing in K–8 classrooms. The writing lessons are organized by grade and topic, and most are only a page or two long. Resources (such as stories or poems) are suggested to help you teach the lesson. This is a great book, but you need to find the resources mentioned to teach the lesson effectively.

Nonfiction Craft Lessons: Teaching Information Writing K–8 by JoAnn Portalupi and Ralph Fletcher (Stenhouse 2001). Equally as good as their first, this book focuses on expository writing techniques.

Favorite Poetry Lessons by Paul Janeczko (Scholastic Trade 1999). This is a wonderful, easy-to-use workbook on how to teach poetry. It is filled with ready-to-use lessons and examples by poet Paul Janeczko.

Expanding Response Journals: In All Subject Areas by Les Parsons (Heinemann 1994). This small handbook is filled with ways to get students to respond through journal writing in all subject areas.

Wondrous Words: Writers and Writing in the Elementary Classroom by Katie Wood Ray (National Council of Teachers of English 1999). This is a beautifully written book outlining how to teach writing at the elementary level. These techniques also work for struggling adolescent writers.

Clearing the Way by Tom Romano (Heinemann 1987). This book talks about how to work with teenage writers (in narrative form).

Assessment

A Measure of Success: From Assignment to Assessment in English Language Arts by Fran Claggett (Boynton/Cook 1996). This book offers research and strategies for how to assign and assess reading and writing.

Parental Involvement

Comics to Classics: A Parent's Guide to Books for Teens and Preteens by A. Reed (International Reading Association 1988). This book is published by the International Reading Association.

The Parent Project: A Workshop Approach to Parent Involvement by James Vopat (Stenhouse 1994). This book provides a way to use a workshop approach to help get parents informed and involved. It was developed in urban bilingual school settings and includes workshop formats in English and Spanish.

Phonics

Phonics They Use by Patricia Cunningham (Addison-Wesley 1999). This book includes theory, research, and practical applications for teaching students about language. It contains lessons on high-frequency words, using word walls, linking spelling and meaning, teaching blends, making words, and more.

Classroom Management/Troubleshooting

Peer Mediation: Finding a Way to Care by Judith Ferrera (Stenhouse 1996). Strategies are offered for forming and maintaining a peer mediation program. This book contains forms, checklists, and standards for forming such a program.

The Teacher's Encyclopedia of Behavior Management by Randall Sprick (Sopris West 1995). This encyclopedia contains a hundred problems and plans for behavior management in grades K–9.

Useful Web Sites
Book Publishers

Atheneum: www.simonsays.com
Bantam Doubleday Dell: www.bdd.com
Crown Publishers: www.randomhouse.com/kids
Dial Books: www.penguinputnam.com
Harcourt Brace: www.harcourtbooks.com
Houghton Mifflin: www.hmco.com
Little, Brown Co.: www.littlebrown.com
Orchard Books: www.grolier.com
Puffin Books: www.penguinputnam.com
Scholastic, Inc.: www.scholastic.com
Stenhouse: www.stenhouse.com

Book Vendors

Advanced Book Exchange (for rare or used books): www.abebooks.com
Alibris (large database for used and out-of-print books): www.alibris.com
Amazon: www.amazon.com
Barnes & Noble: www.bn.com
Bibliofind (for used and out-of-print books): www.bibliofind.com
The Big Link: www.booksearch.com
Bookfinder (for out-of-print books): www.bookfinder.com
The Book Wire Index: www.bookwire.com/index/booksellers.html

The World Wide Web Virtual Library (huge list of on-line stores):
www.comlab.ox.ac.uk/archive/publishers/bookstores.html

Literature and Reading

"Best Books of the Year" (School Library Journal):
www.slj.com/articles/articles/articlesindex.asp
Book Adventure (book club for kids): www.bookadventure.org
Bookhive (children's book reviews): www.bookhive.org/bookhive.htm
Book Links (list of children's literature published by ALA):
www.ala.org/BookLinks/
Booktalks Quick and Simple (book talks listed by subject, title, and author):
www.rms.concord.k12.nh.us/booktalks
Center for the Study of Books in Spanish for Children & Adolescents:
www.coyote.csusm.edu/campus_canter/csb/english
"Choices" Awards: Students and teachers vote on their favorites (part of
International Reading Association): www.reading.org/choices/
International Reading Association (IRA): www.reading.org
and www.readingonline.org
READ Magazine (Weekly Reader publication):
www.weeklyreader.com/wrstore

Reading Aloud

Do's and Don'ts of Reading Aloud:
161.31.208.51/ched/johnson/guidelin.htm
Read Aloud Strategies: clercenter.gallaudet.edu/Literacy/readit45.htm

Research

ALFY (kid-friendly): www.alfy.com/ALFY
Ask Jeeves for Kids (students can type in a complete sentence):
www.ajkids.com
Britannica: www.ebig.com
The Library of Congress: www.loc.gov/
Metacrawler (queries other search engines to find everything!):
www.metacrawler.com
National Geographic Xpeditions (great for research in history and geogra-
phy): www.nationalgeographic.com/xpeditions
Searchopolis (for kids): www.searchopolis.com
Study Web (extensive list of links to education research sorted by grade
level): www.studyweb.com
Yahooligans (for kids): www.yahooligans.com

Teaching

AskERIC (Educational Resources Information Center):
www.askeric.org/about

The Chalkboard (information on materials, lesson plans, and grants):
www.thechalkboard.com/

Cyberguides (based on California Language Arts State Standards):
www.sdcoe.k12.ca.us/score/cyberguide/html

Education Place (created by Houghton Mifflin/elementary):
www.eduplace.com/

Education Week (weekly newspaper on politics, curriculum, editorials,
etc.): www.edweek.com

The English Companion (created by Jim Burke, a high school teacher in
California; gives NCTE news, censorship alerts, test-taking tips, and
articles): www.englishcompanion.com

Teachers Helping Teachers (lesson plans from all content areas):
www.pacificnet.net/~mandel/

Teachnet (information on all aspects of teaching): www.teachnet.com/

Teacher's Online Notebook (lists up-to-date educational links):
www.technology4u.com/ton/

Writing

Creative Writing for Teens: kidswriting.about.com/teens/kidswriting/
index.htm?COB=home&PID=2773

Guide to Grammar and Writing:
webster.commnet.edu/HP/pages/darling/grammar.htm

Merlyn's Pen (Children's and adolescent writing): www.merlynspen.com

Outta Ray's Head Writing Lessons: www3.sympatico.ca/ray.saitz/writing.htm

Teen Ink (publishes adolescent writing): www.TeenInk.com

Write Environment: writeenvironment.com/linksto.html

Write Site: www.writesite.org/default.htm

Organizations and Catalogs

Organizations

American Library Association (ALA)
50 E. Heron Street
Chicago, IL 60611
(312) 944-6780
(800) 545-2433
www.ala.org

International Reading Association (IRA)
800 Barksdale Road
P.O. Box 8139
Newark, DE 19714-8139
(302) 731-1600
(800) 336-READ
www.reading.org

National Council of Teachers of English
1111 W. Kenyon Road
Urbana, IL 61801-1096
(217) 328-3870
(800) 369-6283
www.ncte.org

Book Clubs

TAB: The Teen Book Club
Scholastic Book Clubs, Inc.
Jefferson City, MO 65102-7503
(800) 724-6527
www.scholastic.com/tab

Troll 6–9 Book Club
Troll Book Clubs
2 Lethbridge Plaza
Mahwah, NJ 07430
(800) 541-1097
www.troll.com

TRUMPET 4–6
The Trumpet Club
P.O. Box 7510
Jefferson City, MO 65102-7510
(800) 826-0110

Catalog Information

Alta Book Center
14 Adrian Court
Burlingame, CA 94010
(800) ALTA/ESL
www.altaesl.com

Listening Library
One Park Avenue
Old Greenwich, CT 06870-1727

(800) 243-4504
www.listeninglib.com

Merlyn's Pen
P.O. Box 910
East Greenwich, RI 02818
(800) 247-2027
www.merlynspen.com

Peachtree Publishers
494 Armour Circle, NE
Atlanta, GA 30324-4088
(800) 241-0113
www.peachtree-online.com

READ Magazine
Weekly Reader Corporation
3001 Cindel Drive
P.O. Box 8007
Delran, NJ 08075-9978
(800) 446-3355
www.weeklyreader.com/wrstore

Recorded Books, Inc.
270 Skipjack Road
Prince Frederick, MD 20678
(800) 638-1304

Scholastic Professional Books
P.O. Box 7502
Jefferson City, MO 65102
(800) 724-6527
www.scholastic.com

Sundance
Middle and High School
Dept. 0503
P.O. Box 1326
Littleton, MA 01460
(800) 343-8204
www.sundancepub.com

Troll Communications
Grades K–8
100 Corporate Drive
Mahwah, NJ 07430
(800) 541-1097
www.troll.com

References

Professional

Allen, Janet. 1995. *It's Never Too Late: Leading Adolescents to Lifelong Literacy.* Portsmouth, NH: Heinemann.

———. 2000. *Yellow Brick Roads: Shared and Guided Paths to Independent Reading 4–12.* Portland, ME: Stenhouse.

Allen, Janet, and Kyle Gonzalez. 1998. *There's Room for Me Here: Literacy Workshop in the Middle School.* Portland, ME: Stenhouse.

Allington, Richard. 2001. *What Really Matters for Struggling Readers: Designing Research-Based Programs.* New York: Longman.

Atwell, Nancie. 1987. *In the Middle: Writing, Reading, and Learning with Adolescents.* Portsmouth, NH: Heinemann-Boynton/Cook.

———. 1991. *Side by Side: Essays on Teaching to Learn.* Portsmouth, NH: Heinemann.

Bacon, Francis. 1996. *Philosophical Studies.* New York: Clarendon Press.

Calkins, Lucy. 2001. *The Art of Teaching Reading.* New York: Longman.

Carter, Candy, and Zora M. Rashkis, eds. 1981. *Ideas for Teaching English in the Junior High and Middle School.* Urbana, IL: National Council of Teachers of English.

Cunningham, Patricia, Dorothy Hall, and Cheryl Sigmon. 2001. *The Teacher's Guide to the Four Blocks: A Multimethod, Multilevel Framework for Grades 1–3.* Greensboro, NC: Carson Dellosa.

Duckworth, Eleanor. 1996. *The Having of Wonderful Ideas and Other Essays on Teaching and Learning.* New York: Teachers College Press.

Duncan, Lois, ed. 1998. *Trapped! Cages of Mind and Body.* New York: Simon & Schuster.

Fletcher, Ralph. 1996. *Breathing In, Breathing Out: Keeping a Writer's Notebook.* Portsmouth, NH: Heinemann.

Fletcher, Ralph, and JoAnn Portalupi. 1998. *Craft Lessons: Teaching Writing K–8.* Portland, ME: Stenhouse.

Fischer, Louis, ed. 1983. *The Essential Gandhi: His Life, Work, and Ideas.* New York: Vintage Books.

Hoff, Benjamin. 1983. *The Tao of Pooh.* New York: Viking.

Holdaway, Don. 1979. *The Foundations of Literacy.* Portsmouth, NH: Heinemann.

Holmes, Oliver Wendell, Jr. 1989 [1943]. *The Mind and Faith of Justice Holmes: His Speeches, Essays, Letters, and Judicial Opinions.* Portland, OR: Booknews.

Johnson, Thomas H., ed. 1976. *The Complete Poems of Emily Dickinson.* Boston: Little, Brown.

Keyes, Ralph. 1993. *Nice Guys Finish Seventh: False Phrases, Spurious Sayings, and Familiar Misquotations.* New York: HarperCollins.

Krashen, Stephen. 1993. *The Power of Reading.* Englewood, CO: Libraries Unlimited.

Mooney, Margaret. 1990. *Reading To, With, and By Children.* Katonah, NY: Richard C. Owen.

Neilsen, Lorri. 1994. *A Stone in My Shoe: Teaching Literacy in Times of Change.* Winnepeg, Manitoba: Peguis.

Ohanian, Susan. 1999. *One Size Fits Few: The Folly of Educational Standards.* Portsmouth, NH: Heinemann.

Paine, Albert Bigelow, ed. 1990. *Mark Twain's Speeches.* New York: Nineteenth Century Club.

Peterson, Ralph. 1992. *Life in a Crowded Place: Making a Learning Community.* Portsmouth, NH: Heinemann.

Pilgreen, Janice. 2000. *The SSR Handbook: How to Organize and Manage a Sustained Silent Reading Program.* Portsmouth, NH: Heinemann.

Ray, Katie Wood. 1999. *Wondrous Words: Writers and Writing in the Elementary Classroom.* Urbana, IL: National Council of Teachers of English.

Sigmon, Cheryl. 2000. *Modifying the Four Blocks for Upper Grades.* Greensboro, NC: Carson Dellosa.

Smith, Frank. 1994. *Understanding Reading: A Psycholinguistic Analysis of Reading and Learning to Read.* Hillsdale, NJ: Lawrence Erlbaum.

———. 1988. *Joining the Literacy Club: Further Essays into Education.* Portsmouth, NH: Heinemann.

Tovani, Cris. 2000. *I Read It, but I Don't Get It: Comprehension Strategies for Adolescent Readers.* Portland, ME: Stenhouse.

Trelease, Jim. 1993. *Read All About It.* New York: Penguin.

———. 2001. *The Read-Aloud Handbook.* New York: Penguin.

Warwick, B. Elley. 1992. *How in the World Do Students Read?* Hamburg, Germany: International Association for the Evaluation of Educational Achievement.

Children's Literature

Bloor, Edward. 1997. *Tangerine*. San Diego, CA: Harcourt Brace.

Blume, Judy. 1974. *Blubber*. Scarsdale, NY: Bradbury Press.

Canfield, Jack, Mark Victor Hanson, Kimberly Kirberger, comps. 1997. *Chicken Soup for the Teenage Soul: 101 Stories of Life, Love, and Learning*. Deerfield Beach, FL: Health Communications.

———. 1998. *Chicken Soup for the Teenage Soul II: 101 More Stories of Life, Love, and Learning*. Deerfield Beach, FL: Health Communications.

———. 2000. *Chicken Soup for the Teenage Soul III: More Stories of Life, Love, and Learning*. Deerfield Beach, FL: Health Communications.

———. Chicken Soup for the Soul Series. Deerfield Beach, FL: Health Communications.

Conford, Ellen. 1994. *I Love You, I Hate You, Get Lost*. New York: Scholastic.

Crutcher, Chris. 1983. *Running Loose*. New York: Greenwillow Books.

Curtis, Christopher Paul. 1995. *The Watsons Go to Birmingham—1963*. New York: Delacorte Press.

DeFelice, Cynthia. 1990. *Weasel*. New York: Macmillan.

Deuker, Carl. 1988. *On the Devil's Court*. Boston: Joy Street Books.

Flake, Sharon. 1998. *The Skin I'm In*. New York: Jump at the Sun/Hyperion Books for Children.

Gallo, Donald R., ed. 1987. *Visions: Nineteen Short Stories by Outstanding Writers for Young Adults*. New York: Delacorte Press.

———. 1997. *No Easy Answers: Short Stories About Teenagers Making Tough Choices*. New York: Delacorte Press.

Haddix, Margaret Peterson. 1996. *Don't You Dare Read This, Mrs. Dunphrey*. New York: Simon & Schuster Books for Young Readers.

Harden, M. 1989. "O Romeo, O, Like, Wow." *Columbus Dispatch,* November 8.

Hoh, Diane. 1993. *Nightmare Hall: The Silent Scream*. New York: Scholastic.

Jennings, P. 1996. "A Mouthful." In *Uncovered! Weird, Weird Stories*. New York: Viking Penguin.

Lowry, Lois. 1993. *The Giver*. Boston: Houghton Mifflin.

Mighty, The. 1998. Produced by Scholastic Productions and directed by Peter Chelson. Miramax Films. Videocassette.

Mills, Claudia. 1998. *Standing Up to Mr. O*. New York: Farrar, Straus and Giroux.

Myers, Walter Dean. 1988. *Scorpions*. New York: Harper & Row.

———. 1996. *Slam!* New York: Scholastic Press.

Paterson, Katherine. 1989. *The Spying Heart*. Onalaska, WI: Lodestar.

Pelzer, David J. 1993. *A Child Called "It."* Omaha, NE: Omaha Press.

———. 1994. *The Lost Boy*. Omaha, NE: Omaha Press.

———. 1999. *A Man Named Dave: A Story of Triumph and Forgiveness*. New York: Dutton.

————. 2000. *Help Yourself: Celebrating the Rewards of Resilience and Gratitude.* New York: Dutton.

Pfeffer, Susan Beth. 1994. *Twice Taken.* New York: Delacorte Press.

Philbrick, Rodman. 1993. *Freak the Mighty.* New York: Scholastic.

————. 1998. *Max the Mighty.* New York: Scholastic.

Rawls, Wilson. 1961. *Where the Red Fern Grows: The Story of Two Dogs and a Boy.* New York: Doubelday.

Rowling, J. K. 2000. *Harry Potter and the Goblet of Fire.* New York: Arthur A. Levine Books.

————. Harry Potter Series. New York: Arthur A. Levine Books.

Spinelli, Jerry. 1984. *Who Put That Hair in My Toothbrush?* Boston: Little, Brown.

————. 1990. *Maniac Magee.* Boston: Little, Brown.

————. 1996. *Crash.* New York: Knopf: Distributed by Random House.

————. 1997. *Wringer.* New York: HarperCollins.

————. 2000. *Stargirl.* New York: Knopf: Distributed by Random House.

Stine, R. L. 1995. *The Cuckoo Clock of Doom.* New York: Scholastic.

————. Goosebumps Series. New York: Scholastic.

Taylor, Mildred D. 2001. *Roll of Thunder, Hear My Cry.* New York: Phyllis Fogelman Books.

Twain, Mark. 1984. *Pudd'nhead Wilson.* New York: Bantam Classics.

Watterson, Bill. Calvin and Hobbes Cartoon Series. Andrew McMeel Publishers.